Ridgway, John
    A fighting chance [by] John Ridgway &
Chay Blyth.   Lippincott, 1967.
    242 p. illus., facsim., map (on lining
papers)

s. G.
52° 17

4.95

A
Fighting
Chance

John Ridgway &
Chay Blyth A
Fighting
Chance

J. B. Lippincott Company | PHILADELPHIA
NEW YORK

1967

Acknowledgements

We should like to thank Ken Gardner and Robert Taylor of The People, Noel Botham of the Daily Sketch and John Austin for their help and encouragement in the writing of this book, and also Lieutenant-Colonel M. A. J. Tugwell, Commanding Officer of the Depot of the Parachute Regiment and Airborne Forces. We are grateful to The Borden Chemical Company (UK) Ltd. for permission to reproduce photographs of English Rose III being made ready for her voyage, and to Syndication International for permission to reproduce two photographs taken from the Haustellum.

To

The Dorymen of Cape Cod
who gave us 'A Fighting Chance'

Contents

CONTENTS

ENDPAPERS: Map showing the voyage of *English Rose III*

Departure

John Ridgway: June 4

JUST before five-thirty on the afternoon of June 4, 1966, I stood on the beach of the little fishing port of Orleans, near Cape Cod, Massachusetts. I could hardly believe my sight or my hearing.

Around me were thousands of people, all shouting my name and that of the short, stocky fellow who stood beside me, Chay Blyth. I looked at Chay and said, 'Can this really be for us?' Chay gave his usual rather shy grin and chuckled, 'Yep—it's all for us.'

It was the kind of scene that one usually associates with the send-off for an ocean-going liner—flags waving, people shouting, boats blowing their sirens. It made me feel a bit idiotic, really. I looked down at the cold, sparkling water to our little boat, *English Rose III*, gleaming in the sunlight. She looked so beautiful, but so small.

An old man with a stick pushed his way through to me and said, 'Are you really going to row across the Atlantic in that? You must be mad, feller—but I wish you the best of luck just the same. You'll need it.'

Well, I suppose it did all seem a bit crazy. But Chay and I had made up our minds. Our departure time was 17.30 and casually we set our watches. Best to look as casual as possible, I remember thinking.

Chay stood there a bit edgy. He did not like all the fuss and wanted to get moving.

'Well,' he said to me, giving me a gentle push in the ribs. 'Are we going or not?'

'Okay,' I replied. 'Let's go now.'

We said a few last words with those nearest to us. They clapped us on the back, pumped our hands—and almost shoved us into the water with their typical American friendly eagerness.

Chay and I went to *English Rose III*. It was a bit tricky settling ourselves down. Chay got in first and as I did so the boat wobbled like mad. I nearly fell overboard and there was laughing from the wall of faces looking down at us.

After a few moments we were in position, one behind the other. Without another word, we both grasped the oars and began to pull. The first few strokes were somewhat unsteady. I caught a crab and so did Chay. I am sure a good many of those watching us must have thought we were up to some kind of poor joke. But Chay and I were never more serious. Our intention was to row to Britain—and we damn well would!

We made good progress through the little harbour, and I know that both of us had a great feeling of pride that we, a couple of Britishers, were doing this thing. I looked around at all the little ships in the harbour. Every deck was lined with waving, cheering people. Bunting rustled in the early evening breeze and the air was filled with blaring hooters. I am not a sentimental sort, but I must confess that I almost had to wipe away a little tear that was beginning to appear and my stomach seemed full of butterflies.

Looking back, it all seems like a dream that happened a thousand years ago. I can hardly believe it is less than six months since we left that harbour. I have to look at newspaper cuttings now to remind me of the details of the departure. But I do not need similar aids to recall the other aspects of that terrible journey across the North Atlantic—for terrible it was. Every hour of every day had its anxieties. It was a battle between us and the sea every inch of the way.

When I think of that voyage I think of the sea. I think of mountains of black-green, white-flecked water, thousands of tons of it, that threatened every second of the way to smash us into oblivion. Of course we had our calm days, but we never knew when that smooth water would suddenly boil into a steaming cauldron of lashing waves.

I dream of being at the top of one of those mountains —forty feet in height and sometimes higher. From the top I gaze terrified across an alpine seascape which is featureless, except for mountains and yet more mountains. I look down into a black abyss, into which our little boat plunges headlong at the speed of an express train, hissing downwards on the ice-like surface of the wave. There is nothing to stop us and Chay and I hold on tight with a prayer on our lips hoping that our plummeting boat will not make a hole in the bottom of the wave that will swallow us up for ever. Suddenly we are at the bottom of the wave and thankfully we are still afloat. We look up. To the back of us and to the front and towering above us are heaving walls of water that are going to crash on top of us, but it does not happen and somehow we find ourselves riding up the side of one of those walls. We climb almost vertically and we wonder if this time the boat is going to turn a backward somersault and hurl us back into the black valley from which we had just come.

Our journey took us ninety-one days and a bit— thirteen weeks that I never want to face again. We fought a hurricane and countless gales. We fought, too, unseen dangers such as huge whales and sharks that we knew were lurking not far beneath the surface. Any one of them, with a flick of the tail, could have turned us over.

11

Many of these creatures swam round us, eyeing us suspiciously as trespassers who should be smashed to pulp. One of them, I thought, was a sea serpent—or at least it had every appearance of one—which came upon us one dark night. Through the ages mariners have returned with tales of such creatures, only to be told that what they had seen was the product of an over-wrought imagination. I can only tell what I saw with my own eyes, and I am no longer a disbeliever.

Since our return many people have asked why we were foolhardy enough to undertake such a dangerous journey. It was apparently without purpose and served only to feed the ego of those attempting the exploit. I suppose this is partly true. Every man dreams of succeeding in such an adventure, secretly nurturing some personal ambition—which in most cases never reaches fruition. Some men are luckier. They climb Everest, pioneer the Poles or become the first to explore the depths of jungles.

It was this deep personal sense of adventure that had to be fulfilled which, I suppose, gave Chay and me the impetus to embark on our journey across the Atlantic. We were not the first to do it. It was in fact accomplished in 1896 by two Norwegian sailors, George Harbo and Frank Samuelson. They made it in the incredible time of sixty-two days and arrived at Le Havre from New York, not surprisingly half dead.

My interest in such an exploit was aroused one day in August 1965 when I was on holiday with my wife, Marie-Christine, at our croft in Scotland. I was shaving one morning and listening to the radio. Jack de Manio, the B.B.C. personality, was interviewing a journalist called David Johnstone about some project he had in mind. I was only half-listening. But suddenly I began to understand. This incredible man Johnstone was actually proposing to row across the Atlantic.

As a serving officer in the Parachute Regiment, I had completed a great number of fitness and survival tests in various parts of the world. Some time before, partnered by a para N.C.O., Sergeant Chay Blyth, I won a canoe race from Reading to London, a distance of 70 miles. But the Atlantic would be a survival test of a different order.

I listened to the rest of the interview with close attention. I could smell bacon and eggs cooking in the kitchen as Marie-Christine prepared breakfast, but food had no interest for me that morning. When my wife called that breakfast was ready I was already strolling across the nearby heather. I wanted to be alone and to think.

That day we went fishing with another couple, and I realise now I must have made a poor companion. I could think of nothing but Johnstone's proposed row. By the time we returned to the croft at the end of the day I had made up my mind to join him. By sheer coincidence, we lived in the same town—Farnham, Surrey. I was determined to talk to him as soon as possible.

When my leave ended I returned to Farnham, obtained Johnstone's telephone number and tried several times to contact him—without success. His mother must have passed on my message, for a few weeks later David suddenly arrived on my doorstep as I was getting ready for a regimental dinner. I recognised his huge, bearded frame immediately. To add to the coincidence of living in the same town, I realised I had met him briefly in Bahrein in 1961.

He outlined the project to me. He told me that he had advertised in *The Times* for volunteers and, it seemed, had already made his choice. He told me that he intended to make the trip with a young man called John Hoare, another journalist, who lived in Leicester. So keen was Hoare to go, said Johnstone, that he even intended to have his appendix out to avoid trouble in that direction in mid-ocean.

I was certainly not prepared to go to such lengths. By the time our conversation came to an end, it was apparent that we both viewed the project in a somewhat different light. I pursued the matter with him no further. We shook hands and he left.

This did not mean that my interest had waned. Indeed, my conversation with Johnstone acted as a spur and I mentioned what was in my mind to a number of people. My intention was to find my own boat—and race Johnstone across the Atlantic.

On Sunday, February 27, 1966, an article about Johnstone's proposed trip appeared in *The People* newspaper. It gave me just the incentive I needed. As I sat reading the paper after lunch I turned to my wife and said, 'This is it. If Johnstone can do it, so can I.'

I sat down with a fellow officer, Captain Colin Thomson, who was willing to join me, and wrote a detailed military appreciation of the situation. It was headed: 'Aim: To win a rowing race across the Atlantic Ocean from the United States of America to the United Kingdom during the summer of 1966.'

From what I knew of Johnstone's intentions, it was clear that I had only about fifty-five days to find myself a boat and fit it out, leaving a couple of weeks for the final preparations in America.

Obviously, I wanted a boat of the utmost seaworthiness and I was convinced that I should have one built by Colin Mudie, the London designer of Johnstone's boat, *Puffin*. The cost of this, I discovered, would be in the region of £2,000. I did not have that much money, so I thought about raising part of it by extending the mortgage on my house in Farnham. As for the rest, I thought I might be able to get a national newspaper interested enough to give me a substantial advance against the outright purchase of publication rights for our story when we returned.

I contacted a number of Fleet Street newspapers. Each time the reaction was that I was foolish to make the attempt and that the last thing an editor wished to do was finance disaster.

The days and weeks went by. I began to despair of ever being able to make the trip. In fact, by the time March came I was beginning to tell my friends that the whole project was off. After all, by that time Johnstone's boat was ready for launching and he had made bookings to take it by sea from Glasgow to Norfolk, Virginia. The position seemed hopeless.

Then, on March 25, when I arrived at my office, a letter awaited me. It was from Hugh Ross, an old friend of mine in Scotland. He knew of my eagerness to find a boat and mentioned in the letter that he thought a boat being made by Bradford Boat Services, Bradford, Yorkshire, might be suitable. It was called the Yorkshire Dory, and its design was based on the dory which for centuries had been used by fishermen off Nova Scotia. I was excited. Perhaps this was the answer!

The factors which appealed to me most were the ship's well-tried sea-worthiness and the cost—a mere £185. At once I phoned the firm, found they had a dory in stock and promptly sent off a cheque for £185.

I could hardly wait for the boat to arrive. At last I was beginning to feel that my plan was really on. Many people I knew rather smirked at what they regarded as a foolhardy adventure. But I was greatly encouraged by Eric Lee, a Services' boat expert, Lieutenant-Colonel M. A. J. Tugwell and Brigadier R. C. Gibbs, D.S.O., M.C., both of the Parachute Regiment, and other fellow officers.

The one snag at that point was that it was clear that Captain Thomson, who helped me draw up the original plan, would not be able to accompany me on the trip because of his susceptibility to seasickness. He had been medically examined and the advice of his doctor was that he should withdraw.

Who could take Colin's place? Time was running out fast. It was imperative that I find a suitable partner quickly. I scouted around Aldershot and sought the help of a great number of old friends. I told them of my need, chatted at length with a great number of people they recommended, but none was suitable. The sort of partner I was looking for had to be fit—very fit. He had to be tough, morally, physically and mentally. He also had to be a person I liked and trusted and could lean on if the occasion should ever arise. In short, I looked for a man in whose hands I might have to place my life. It was a tall order, I agree.

Suddenly, on April 16, just as I was preparing to go home for the week-end, there was a knock at my office door.

'Come in,' I called.

The door opened and in marched the spruce figure of Sergeant Chay Blyth. I knew him well. He was my platoon sergeant in '3 Para' for three years. Together we had won the Reading–London canoe race. I was happy to see him again and we shook hands.

As we chatted, I knew that here was the man who would be ideal for the kind of adventure I proposed. I had known it from the beginning—but how could I ask him to accompany me? Blyth was married. It would have been unfair to put the proposition to him or to any other married man.

Casually he mentioned the project. He said he had heard that I had at last found a boat and that a fellow N.C.O., Sergeant Surman, under the direction of Eric Lee, was modifying the craft slightly in his spare time in the depot's cinema.

'Yes,' I said. 'I hope we shall be under way in a few weeks' time.'

'Who is going with you, sir?' asked Blyth.

'Nobody yet. I'm still looking for somebody.'

Blyth replied, 'Can I come, sir? I know you've been asking a lot of people. I was wondering why you hadn't asked me.'

I explained that I had approached only unmarried men.

Blyth grinned. 'I've talked this over with Maureen already,' he said. 'She says I can go.'

My heart thumped. I would have to speak to his wife, of course. But supposing it came off? I could hardly believe my good luck. There was no better man for such a job as this. I told Blyth I would contact him and dashed home to tell Marie-Christine, who knew Blyth, the good news.

'Good,' she said. 'I knew all along that Chay Blyth was the man for you. I'm delighted he's going—if Mrs. Blyth agrees.'

A few days later the four of us met at my house and there was no doubt in my mind that Mrs. Maureen Blyth was one hundred per cent. behind her husband and the decision he had made. Everything had at last begun to go well and I was delighted.

In her sea trials at Portsmouth, the dory—or *English Rose III* as I had named her—came through with a higher standard of worthiness than I had expected. To cap everything, I was informed that the Ministry of Defence (Army) was prepared to support us to the hilt by giving both Blyth and myself as much unpaid leave as we needed to complete the trip.

To prepare ourselves for the ardours of the voyage ahead of us, Blyth and I embarked on a course of fitness and training, even more intensive than the Para's unusually high standard with which we were both more than familiar.

Neither of us ever smoked or drank and every day we ran at least three miles, in addition to workouts in the gymnasium. Chay swam a lot and the last thing I did every night before going to bed was perform fifty press-ups on the dining-room floor.

Chay and I were not just fit. We were very fit—and full of confidence that if our rivalry with the Johnstone camp became a race, then we stood a good chance of winning.

It was something of a setback, therefore, when I read that Johnstone and Hoare, together with *Puffin*, had sailed for America on the *United States* on April 27, two weeks ahead of schedule. Well, there were no rules for this race. If they wanted to jump the gun—good luck to them.

A few days later, on May 4, I drove through the night to Glasgow, followed by *English Rose III* on the back of a lorry, and left her there for shipment to Boston. I had already grown closely attached to the little boat and I was sorry to leave her there, but there were still a number of military commitments to deal with before Blyth and I were able to depart for the States ourselves.

On May 17, Blyth and I said goodbye to our wives and left London Airport for Ottawa, having scrounged a couple of spare seats in an R.A.F. aircraft. I was filled with a strange excitement, for at last I could really believe, after all the setbacks, that our venture was really under way.

From Ottawa we took a Greyhound coach to Boston, a long journey that was made worse by the fact that we both had to stand part of the way. The Americans we met were curious to know if we were tourists. When I explained that we had come over by air to row back, their incredulity was quite something.

'Man—do you mean that? All that way in a little boat? You must be joking.'

By the time we reached Boston, I was feeling considerable pain in my left foot, which definitely was not funny. As I got off the bus with my luggage, a burning pain shot through my leg and my foot felt uncomfortably swollen. In fact, I stumbled and would have fallen if Chay Blyth had not steadied me by taking my arm.

'What's the matter?' he said. 'Not trouble, I hope?'

'I don't think it's much,' I said—but when I got to our hotel and removed my shoe, I became thoroughly alarmed. My left foot was twice its normal size and had turned blue.

A close examination revealed that a small cut which I had incurred while on a training run a week or so before had apparently turned septic. I got in touch with the American Naval authorities, who were aware of our arrival, and a doctor came to see me. He took one look at the foot and ordered me to be taken at once to Boston's Chelsea Naval Hospital.

So my first night in America was spent in a hospital bed with a penicillin drain into my veins from a bottle suspended above my head. It was a most embittering experience. There I was, helpless and not knowing when I would get better, while five hundred miles south in Norfolk, Virginia, last-minute preparations were being made for *Puffin*'s departure.

My morale hit rock bottom on Saturday, May 21. A nurse came to my bed to change the penicillin bottle at about lunchtime and whispered to me, 'Have you heard? *Puffin*'s just sailed.'

I had to make up my mind whether to insist on my discharge and get started or to wait until the doctors decided I was fit enough to leave. I thought of poor old Chay and all the arrangements he would have to make on his own while I was laid up. There were stores to buy

and the addition of nine inches on the gunwale, to increase the sea-worthiness of *English Rose III*, to be
supervised.

Despite this I thought it would be prudent to stay
here until I was better. I had never before had poison in
my system and I knew that, even with the best of treatment, it was always possible that the condition would
reassert itself once we were under way.

On May 24, after almost a week in hospital, the doctors decided I was fit enough to leave, by which time
Puffin had a start of three days. I wondered how far behind her we would eventually be.

But the winds were not in *Puffin*'s favour. In fact,
after a week at sea she was still offshore. I was heartened.
I knew I could take my time in making final preparations—and still catch *Puffin*.

In the course of the next few days, I had the most
enormous amount of help from a host of fine American
friends whose kindness I shall never forget. Complete
strangers would approach us with gifts of every descrip-
tion for the voyage. Watches, cameras, clothing—their
generosity was overwhelming. Why did we decide to
leave from Cape Cod? Simply because Johnstone and
Hoare said they were leaving from there, then they
changed their minds and went to Norfolk, which was
nearer to the Gulf Stream. We would have followed
them, but we did not have the money.

Since I was a boy I had read about the marvellous
fishermen of Cape Cod who had used dories years ago
and I was amazed to find that some were still alive—in
their eighties and nineties. They were wonderful old
men who knew all about the sea and the dory; some had
been in dories in 70-m.p.h. hurricanes and had got back
safely. I think the only good people in this world are the
people who know about suffering, and those dorymen
knew what suffering was all about. I warmed to them.

One old man would take us out on Pleasant Bay to give us rowing lessons. We had the idea that you had to lean far forward and then really pull and lean far backward. But he and the other men said that if you are going to row for long, the idea is to concentrate on just keeping the boat moving. You should not lean back and you must row with shorter strokes. And if you pulled too hard, you would raise blisters.

The fishermen were really excited about our trip and they would tell us, 'We know you guys are sincere and we want to give you a chance—a fighting chance.' And that is what they did. Apart from building up the sides of the boat, they put in thick pieces of oak to reinforce the boat—and they advised us not to use a keel.

They decided this sitting round an old stove. After several hours' deliberation, they announced, 'You don't want a keel. We've come out against that.'

They said a keel would stop the dory from slipping off the waves as it was meant to. I took their advice. They knew.

And then there were the people in the town who would give us anything. A typical example was an American who came up to me with a ten-shilling note one day while I was working on the boat.

'Take this, son. I won a lot of money in England and this is one of the notes. I hope it brings you luck too.'

Chay and I had become celebrities of some note. We were mentioned on news bulletins and numerous articles about us appeared in the newspapers. Wherever we went in the little fishing towns of Orleans and Chatham we were recognised and stopped in the street with messages of good luck—and many offers of material help. Tins of food were showered on us, and far more equipment than we could ever have used. Johnny Stello, Charlie Moore, Skip Norgeot—these are just some of the names of the many fine friends we found in Orleans and in neighbouring Chatham.

When some of the local dorymen discovered that Chay did not know the first thing about boats or the sea, they went out of their way to teach him. Chay speaks with a broad Scots accent—he comes from Hawick—and I shall always remember the day when a local fisherman asked him about his sea experience.

'Experience?' said Chay. 'I've got none—unless you can call a day trip across the Channel and a pleasure steamer up the Clyde, experience.'

The local did not understand a word and asked Chay to repeat what he had said. Chay did so—but the fisherman walked away shaking his head none the wiser.

We spent upwards of fourteen hours a day preparing 'Rosie' as we affectionately began to call her. Apart from the raising of the gunwales at Orleans, extra buoyancy compartments had been installed and turtle decks fitted before leaving England. There was no cabin such as the *Puffin* had, but there was a U-frame over which we could fix a canvas canopy as a shelter.

We packed every spare inch with three hundred pounds of dehydrated food, mainly curry and rice, enough to last for eighty days—and stowed 120 gallons of water in polythene bags. The final touch came from the Cape Codders themselves. One of them screwed a little brass plaque into the door of one of the watertight compartments. It read: 'Oh God, thy sea is so great and my boat is so small.'

At last she was ready and both Chay and I stood back to admire this little craft which was to take us on such a long journey. It was a rather emotional moment for both of us.

On June 3 we made our decision. We would sail next day. As word of this swept through the town, well-wishers descended upon our small hotel to wish us good luck. We went to bed early that night and slept well. Next morning we were up at six, washed and shaved and were ready to put to sea on the afternoon tide.

The crowds gathered; there were cheers and shouts of God-speed. And at exactly 17.30 we were away. It was a moment of tremendous excitement for both of us. I think we were both so full we could hardly talk.

There was another reason for our silence. We were both most anxious that, due to our unfamiliarity with the boat, we should not make fools of ourselves. Apart from the few lessons he had received from the local dorymen, Chay was a complete novice.

Alongside rowed two whalers filled with sea scouts.

'Blimey,' said Chay. 'Look at them. They look as if they could row the Pacific as well.'

An armada of small boats followed us out of the harbour. Slowly we drew away from land and within a few minutes we felt we were really out at sea.

Steadily we pulled at the oars. Even after half an hour or so I began to get a slight ache in the arms and the unaccustomed action of rowing gave me a pain in my legs, so full was the boat with stores.

I asked Chay how he felt. He replied with a chuckle that was swept away in the freshening evening breeze, 'Champion! How are you?'

I do not think I replied. At that moment I think I was overwhelmed with the enormity of the task in which I had involved us.

Our friends in the small boats gradually fell astern until, after half an hour, only Fred Kaplin, who we had got to know so well, was with us in the *Little Darlin'*. After a few more minutes he leaned over the side, waved and shouted, 'Good luck, boys.' It was a sad moment as he turned for home and, as dusk began to fall, we found ourselves quite alone.

Our intention was to row until about midnight and

then drop anchor for a few hours. There were a number of reasons for this. We did not want our progress influenced by the changing tide so near to the coast, and also I felt it necessary that we should have a few hours to collect our thoughts and sleep.

I am no psychologist, but I reasoned that it was not until we were actually at sea that we would feel the full impact of the strange new world we had entered.

Those who have been to sea, perhaps on a voyage, will more readily understand that, however comfortable one's shipboard conditions, there is a difference of routine as compared with the land that takes a little getting used to. Imagine what it is like then, to be on a tiny boat which for many weeks to come is to be your living room, your dining room, your bedroom and your bathroom. A place where two men are to live together, neither one enjoying a vestige of privacy from the other, and each knowing that every weakness, every failure, every shortcoming is going to be exposed to the full.

I think I have a little veneer—which in Army slang can perhaps be reduced to a coarser but more descriptive term—and I think often I am able to cover up my mistakes. In a small boat where two men are living together, this is impossible, as I quickly discovered.

We had been rowing only about three hours when I thought that I should reset the rudder slightly. I shipped my oars and made to bend forward to carry out the alteration when I changed my mind and resumed my seat, but took the opportunity of the brief respite to wipe my brow.

'What's up?' said Chay, still pulling strongly at his pair of oars.

'Oh, nothing,' I replied. 'Just a bit hot, that's all. Wiping the sweat away.'

Chay turned his head towards me. 'I thought you were going to change the direction of the boat,' he said.

'Well, as a matter of fact, I did think about it,' I told him.

The matter was left there, but at once I recognised the first signs of an extraordinary affinity that was already springing up between us. Not just the closeness of a friendship and a strong sense of camaraderie that was bound to develop between us if we were to survive, but something more than that. It was the kind of closeness of relationship that, I suppose, in normal circumstances can only evolve between a pair of identical twins.

I have not been married to my wife, Marie-Christine, long—two years—but often I find we say the same things at the same time. I suppose it can be explained as a kind of telepathy; it was certainly developing between Chay and myself.

Gradually on that first day at sea, darkness closed in until there was nothing between Chay, 'Rosie' and me but the heaving sea, the sound of the breaking waves and the heavens. I felt lonely and frightened. The feeling came on me suddenly and somewhat unexpectedly because although I had considered these possibilities in moments of private thought before leaving, I did not really expect to be affected by anything other than physical discomfort. Now I found that my mind was the active part of my being, the act of rowing quickly becoming a physical process which dissolved in its own monotony.

I still had the pains in my arms and legs and my hands were a trifle sore, but I felt that, until I became more accustomed to the technique of our laborious task, I could depend on the fullest effort from Chay, who seemed cheerfully to carry on without complaint or, indeed, without any great effort. I marvelled at his cheerfulness, his strength and his apparent lack of worry. Of course, I knew that he would be thinking many of the things which were already going through my mind. If so, he was doing a great job of concealing any anxiety.

After three hours' rowing Chay felt thirsty and suggested I carry on while he obtained a drink of water for himself. He asked if I wanted one, but I simply shook my head. I could hardly speak because the steady movement of the boat had built up an increasing feeling of sickness within me and I wanted to vomit.

Chay wasted no time in getting back to his rowing position and for the next few hours we made steady progress in a sea that was getting steadily rougher. Both of us searched continually for some signs of the life that we had left behind, and I think we both secretly hoped that one of our fishermen friends from Orleans who we had got to know so well, would suddenly come up on us and drawl a cheerful, 'Well—hello there.'

It was a kind of homesickness, 1 suppose, for the place and its people, but it was staved off and we continued in our solitude and with our warm memories. Four times we spotted the lights of nearby shipping and two of the boats came closer to investigate. Figures moved about on deck and there were curious looks through the night at the two strange beings who were rowing to nowhere— from nowhere. No shouts were exchanged and the boats veered and went on their way.

I asked Chay how he felt. 'Great,' he replied, 'but what about having a blow for a couple of minutes? We're not going to row like this all bloomin' night, are we?'

'Are you getting tired?' I asked, perhaps a little irritated by what I thought at that time to be a somewhat mutinous tone in his voice.

'No,' he said. 'I'm not. But you kept telling me before we started that it was important to conserve our energies. That was the phrase you used—conserve the energies. Well, what about it?'

I suddenly realised that, of course, Chay was absolutely right to make a very sensible suggestion—and also to unwittingly challenge at this early stage of our trip the implicit idea that I was the only one who could make decisions. It was a partnership with dual and equal authority—this I had made clear to him from the moment he walked into my office at the Aldershot para depot. At the same time there must also have been in our relationship at that early stage of our voyage the feeling that I was the boss, if only because I could boast of experience with boats, whereas Chay could not.

I was glad that Chay had spoken up and I told him so. 'Of course,' I agreed. 'Let's have a blow for a couple of minutes.' And there and then we decided that, so far as possible for the rest of the trip, we would each take up to five minutes off after every fifty minutes of rowing.

Both of us then shipped our oars and we drifted silently into the night. It gave us the chance to have a stretch and massage muscles back to life, and to have a chat about procedure and the general running of the boat. We had already agreed that we would drop our sea anchor at about midnight because we were still only a few miles out and, if we were not careful, would probably be swept back by the changing current swirling around that part of the American coastline.

We resumed rowing for another hour and a half, then I peered at my luminous watch and told Chay it was time to call a halt. I think both of us were pleased about this. I certainly was. I felt tired—and I felt terribly seasick. I had done my best to control the feeling, but I could no longer.

As I dropped the anchor with a plop into the dark water a few inches below us, I felt a wave of relief mixed with nausea to which I just had to give vent. I leaned over the side of the steadily rocking boat and was sick. I wondered desperately what Chay thought of me. I was supposed to be the seaman and he was the landlubber who never before in his life had been to sea. Was he wishing he had never come with me? Was he regarding me with a look of scorn?

I turned and looked at him. He was lying back in the bottom of the boat, his arms folded on his chest, his lips pursed in a silent whistle, and on his face a look of utter bliss. At that moment, as I turned to empty once again my already empty stomach, I was filled with admiration for the cool, quiet stolidity of the man I had chosen to come with me. It was more than that. It was a feeling of gratitude.

Chay suggested a bite to eat and a drop of cocoa to drink. 'You'll feel better after that,' he said. It was a suggestion I considered for only a second or two and told him that anything inside me would only make me feel worse.

'I don't feel so hot,' said Chay. 'I feel a bit seasick too —but I'm going to have a cup of cocoa and some of that bread and ham they gave us before we left.'

In no time he had struck a match and the blue flame of our little butane gas stove was casting its dancing shadows around the inside of our boat.

My feeling of sickness left me as I watched Chay prepare a meal for himself, and it gave way to a feeling of happiness to think that the very normality of preparing a meal was at least one link with the civilisation we had left. I realised that, as the days passed, the strangeness of our existence would go and that we would contrive a system of living that in time would become quite normal to us. Rowing would be as natural as driving a car, working the pump and bailing out as natural as watering the garden.

I was not too sure about sleeping on the hard boards in the bottom of our boat. This was an experience yet to come, but I felt so tired that I was sure that unconsciousness would soon overtake me and I would not notice the discomforts of our cramped sleeping positions. There was no room to stretch out fully. The nearest to recumbency that we could possibly achieve was to wriggle into a half-sitting, half-lying position with the knees drawn up.

This we did and, with the small canvas canopy over us to protect us if only in a small way from the wind and the spray, we settled down in the darkness and drifted into a fitful sleep.

'Thy sea is so great'

Chay Blyth: June 5–12

My face was pressed into a jumble of provisions; my heels were tucked somewhere behind my thighs. I looked at my hands, clutching at the thin space blanket. They were cold and stiff. I tried wiggling my fingers and they didn't seem to want to grip any more. The boat lurched, and so did my stomach. I could feel bruises all over my body from where 'Rosie' had been rolling through the night.

I have always enjoyed sleeping, and I made up my mind, as I lay there, that I would have to devise a more comfortable way of doing it. The thought of spending a couple of months being squeezed, like a human concertina, between the boat's sides, was agonising.

But at least we were on our way. No more waiting and wondering. No more interviews and advice. What we did not know we would have to learn the hard way.

I turned over, ever so slowly, and sat up. John was squatting at the other end of the boat, a blanket wrapped round his shoulders. There were red circles around his eyes and his cheeks were the shade of seaweed.

'So you're finally awake,' he said.

'You look awful,' I said. 'Are you all right?'

He did his best to smile, but it turned to a grimace half-way, and a moment later he was leaning over the side, spewing into the ocean. I felt sorry for him. But I knew that if I showed it he would only be embarrassed. I also knew that if I watched him much longer I would be hanging over the side myself. So I whistled, as loudly as I could, to shut out the noises from his 'quarters' and set about preparing our first breakfast at sea.

Life, I thought, was ironic. John was the experienced sailor. I had never been to sea before. John had been unable to take Captain Thomson with him on the trip because of the captain's seasickness. Now John was out of action for the same reason, and I realised that I would have to insist on rowing back to shore unless his sickness cleared up quickly.

I couldn't row the Atlantic single-handed, and I was determined not to let our pride warp our judgement when it came to making a decision. Neither of us had any illusions. From the start we had agreed that there was no room on board for a passenger. John was the seaman, the navigator, and, as far as this went, I accepted his judgement without question. I watched the kettle boil and hoped I would not be forced to deliver an ultimatum neither of us would like.

I imagined what my mates in Aldershot would say if they could see us after just one night at sea. They would probably laugh like hell and call for a couple of stretchers.

John seemed to be better now. He was sitting up, taking in great lungsful of air. If we have to turn back, I thought, I hope it's you that makes the decision. After all, it was his venture and I didn't want to mess it up.

Breakfast was gloomy. A thick mist had closed in during the night and I could almost feel it pressing 'Rosie' down deeper into the water. John forced down some orange juice, biscuits and rice pudding, choking on every mouthful. But he looked more human and by five o'clock I had washed and stowed away our pressure cooker and was ready to start rowing.

'Okay Number One. Let's get at it.'

We rowed eastwards, for two hours, in silence. Only the slapping of the waves and the creaking of the oars disturbed our thoughts.

Twice I tried to start a conversation with John, but he only answered with a grunt. He had been sick again shortly after breakfast, and I think he needed all his concentration to go on rowing at all.

Even the sight of a huge aircraft-carrier, sliding past through the mist half a mile away, brought only a single, muttered comment from him. We decided later that it must have come from Boston and was on its way to pick up the two American astronauts due to splash down in the Atlantic the following day.

I missed the cheerful, friendly chatter of the men of Cape Cod and could not have felt more lonely if I had been in space myself.

'Let's try to get Cape Cod on the radio,' I suggested.

For ten minutes I cranked away at the hand generator while John repeated our position. Silence. Not a crackle. We looked at each other and I knew we both realised the enormity of our aloneness.

Was anybody bothering to listen for us? The cranking was using up a lot of my energy, but we tried twice more during the morning. Still nothing, so we gave it up for good. It was not until three months later that we heard that the local fishermen had received our full message and had beamed a lengthy reply.

That day we rowed for eight hours. I always rowed in the stern position, as we had decided that John should watch the compass and I would judge the oncoming waves. When one of us rowed alone it was always in the bow position, because of the compass and, of course, it was easier to control the boat single-handed from there.

Sunday, June 5 was for me a day to be pushed into the past as quickly as possible. It was a day of high spirits and heart-twisting depression.

By midday John had got over the worst of his seasickness, but we were both too exhausted to talk. The water was almost flat, and without bothering to put out the sea anchor we flopped down at our respective ends of the boat. Already half asleep I curled into the yoga-like position I had to take up to fit between the boat's sides, and then blanked out for five hours.

When I woke the mist had vanished completely. John had removed his track-suit top and was in his tee shirt rummaging among our provisions.

'On your feet, shipmate,' he said. 'I've just called for a vote and you were nominated as cook. If you fancy a decent steak you'd better get the stove going.'

The sleep had acted like a tonic on him. As I massaged the cramp out of my knees he stood up and began a series of arm and stomach exercises. The sight of him standing there in that small boat in the middle of nowhere, quite unconcernedly going through an army physical training work-out, settled any doubts I had about our going on. Here again was that same John Ridgway I made my offer to weeks ago in Depot headquarters. I hadn't misjudged my man.

For the first time since we embarked I began to enjoy myself. It took only a few minutes to set up the little French gas cooker and soon two juicy steaks were sizzling in the pan.

The steaks had been a final farewell gift from Charlie Moore, a wealthy Orleans councillor who had befriended us in Cape Cod. He told us they were from his personal herd at Milwaukee. Wherever they came from, they were delicious.

'Quite the best steak I've ever eaten,' said John.

By the time our plates were being scraped clean we were joking and swopping yarns as though we were at a family picnic on the Surrey downs.

Our high spirits did not last very long. By mid-afternoon the breeze had freshened to a strong wind and more and more often our oar blades failed to dip the water as 'Rosie' rolled and see-sawed from wave to wave. I flinched every time a big, sharp-topped wave crunched against the bow, and then waited for my stomach to drop, as it boiled whitely along the sides and flicked the stern skywards in passing.

My eyes smarted with the spray and tears streamed down my cheeks, joining the sea water already probing the neck of my track suit.

Then it began to pour with rain, great sheeted gusts of it that turned the sea to leaping foam as far as the eye could see. John rested on his oars and endeavoured to make himself heard.

'It's no use trying to go on in this. We'll only end up breaking an oar,' he shouted.

'Or our heads,' I yelled back. 'Let's get the oars shipped away and the canopy up.'

While I secured the big oars in place along the sides and unfolded the canvas hood, John clambered to the bow and fastened the sea anchor in place. Then we crawled in at the open end of the hood and tried to sleep.

The canopy did not quite cover the boat and suddenly in the gap between the canvas and the side I spotted a cluster of lights about half a mile away. I called John and together we stared out into the darkness.

'From the way it's moving it must be a ship,' he said.

Gradually, as it came closer, we could make out the shape of a huge liner. It looked awful in the dark. I was sure it was heading straight for us and grabbed John's arm.

'I don't care how rough it is. I think we ought to get the oars out and start rowing otherwise that thing is going to run straight into us.'

It was the first time I had ever seen a ship in the dark and it terrified me. The wind was blowing from that direction and I could even hear the deep throbbing of its engines.

'There's nothing at all to worry about,' John told me. 'I doubt if it will come within three hundred yards of us, and even if it came right alongside I don't think it would force us under. It's a big boat and the bow wave would be strong enough to push us to one side before the bow actually touched us. The little boats are the ones to worry about.'

'Well, I'm worried about this one,' I said. 'And I'm keeping my fingers crossed.'

I kept my eyes fixed on the lights. There seemed to be acres of them. After what might have been an hour—but what John said was a couple of minutes—the liner began to grow smaller and less distinct. Only then did I began to breathe more easily. But I did not relax fully until I had seen the last light disappear over the horizon.

Before going to sleep I made sure the torch and fog-horn were very close at hand. John was probably right, but I was not prepared to take any chances.

Several times during that night I woke to discover the horrors I was dreaming about were real. We were badly overladen, and water slopped over the sides every few minutes. Twice I woke to find myself clinging to the seat yelling at John to hold on. But he did not stir once all that night.

The sea anchor helped to steady us a little, but we seemed to have swung broadside on to the waves, and every time one caught us the boat half turned on its side and started to slide down into the trough. Then suddenly we would jolt twenty feet into the air as the next wave reached us.

Wet and afraid I crouched under the dark, stuffy

canopy and hoped that thinking of my wife and home would bring some comfort. I remembered the times Maureen and I had been to church together and realised for the first time just how off-hand I had been in my dealings with God and my religion. I had never been a very regular churchgoer and when I went at all it was just to keep Maureen company. But on that second night at sea as I clung, tired, wet and frightened to the boat's side I knew without any doubt at all that it would be only with God's help and guidance that John and I would come through this adventure alive.

If either one of us were to be taken ill or fell overboard it would take hours, perhaps days, for anyone to come to our assistance—even assuming that someone did pick up the signal from our emergency 'mayday' radio beacon. The only one who could really help us was God, and I prayed to him that night to look kindly on our boat.

I am sure John must have been thinking along similar lines during the night, for as we huddled together the following morning to eat breakfast he looked up and said, 'I suggest we screw our St. Christopher medals to the stern.' Father McMann had given us these, and it made us feel much happier to see the two tiny silver discs fastened against 'Rosie's' paintwork.

By dawn the wind had dropped and the waves gradually became less threatening. For several hours we rowed steadily towards the East and by mid-afternoon I noticed that the rubbing strips had begun to wear on the oars. Fortunately our hands were standing up to the punishment far better, and there was, as yet, no hint of soreness or blisters.

At noon we paused for John to take a sighting with the sextant. He made a rapid calculation in his notebook and I knew straight away from the grim set of his face that something was seriously wrong.

'If I took the sighting right, then it means we are already miles north of our real course,' he said. 'I knew the wind was pushing us north, but this is even worse than I feared. It means that if we don't row harder, or if the wind doesn't change, then we are almost certain to be washed up on the Nova Scotia coast.'

Our morale, low as it was, plummeted to rock bottom, and as the wind—still from the south-west—steadily increased to gale force we resigned ourselves to what seemed almost definite failure. All that day and in the days that followed we expected to come within sight of land at any moment, but never did.

At the time we could not work it out. But later we discovered that John had been working out our position wrongly. When the expected coastline failed to rise above the northern horizon he grew certain that he was using the sextant incorrectly. After two days of careful thinking and rechecking his calculations he decided that instead of shooting the sun at noon—taken from the radio pips of Eastern standard time—he would take his sighting when the sun reached its highest point in the sky. It worked. Just those few minutes in timing had given us a completely false latitude reckoning and placed us several degrees north of our true position.

But the chance of being blown ashore was not our only danger on that evening of June 6. By six o'clock the waves were the height of a double-decker bus, rising way above our boat. It was hopeless to go on rowing with a full gale blowing, and despite what we believed to be a desperate need to better our position, and haul 'Rosie' further south, we elected to stow the oars.

Our reaction to the bad weather was just like that of two scared ostriches. I sat next to John in the centre of the boat and helped him draw the canvas canopy over our heads to shut out our view of the sea. Soaked to the skin and shivering with cold and fear we sat face to face, trying to block our ears against the thunder of breaking waves. Two huge waves broke right over the boat and hundreds of pounds of water landing on the canopy flattened us both along the bottom boards.

'Oh God, I think we're going to go under,' I shouted. But John wasn't going to let the sea finish us off that quickly. He threw back the canvas and jerked me to my feet.

'We won't if you start bailing out,' he cried.

I grabbed our bailers, two buckets secured to the side by lengths of string, and began scooping the water—half a gallon at a time—over the side. In a few seconds John had the pumps going and soon we could actually see the water level going down.

It was a terrifying half hour, but the experience at least gave us both a lasting confidence in our boat. 'Rosie' could stand up to whatever nature decided to chuck against her, but of our own ability to stand up to this kind of punishment for any length of time, I was still far from certain.

In the next twenty-four hours we had plenty of opportunity to think about the future and the further hazards that must lie ahead. Reading now what I wrote in my log on that day I mentally kick myself for the tragic error we both made, largely due to our inexperience and fear.

'Nothing but sleep and eat today,' I wrote. 'The wind is too strong to row with to be able to make any headway. We put the sea anchor out and just waited.'

If only we had had the courage to continue rowing, instead of just staying doggo and drifting in those coastal gales, we could have lopped days off our journey. But the nearness of those twenty-foot waves, and the thought of what they could do to us if we were caught off balance, made cowards of us both.

A few weeks later, in a braver moment, we decided to

carry on rowing during a south-westerly gale. 'Rosie' fairly sped across the water. And in those periods we calculated we had covered more than twice the daily distance achieved in calmer seas. By persevering at the oars in those early days we could have reached our immediate goal—the Gulf Stream—a good four days sooner than we actually did.

To make matters worse John discovered, during a routine check late that afternoon, that our sea anchor had been carried away in the gale. God knows how far we were blown to the north that day. We went to our sleeping positions too worried and too depressed to discuss it.

We woke shortly before dawn after a freezing night, with heavy rain that had pounded the canvas like tribal drums, keeping me for hours from sleeping. Almost straight away John spotted a distant light, flashing in a regular sequence, towards the North-west, and this brought all our worries of the previous night crowding back.

Remembering the reports of how David Johnstone and John Hoare had been blown back to within a mile of the shore a week after they set off, we were convinced that this was a lighthouse, and it confirmed John's fear that we were being blown towards the northern coast of the Gulf of Maine.

Even after spending three months in the Atlantic I can still hardly believe the astonishing speed with which weather conditions changed. Early on the morning of June 8 the wind died away. Within a few hours the sea was as flat as Loch Lomond in mid-summer, and we were rowing steadily through a dead calm in thick fog.

For the second day running John was unable to take a sighting, and even though he was calculating our position wrongly, it would have given us considerable relief to have had some idea of where we were.

I prayed for a ship to come alongside and give us our position—but when we did hear one approaching sounding its fog-horn I was terrified. I yanked in my oars and almost knocked John off his seat in my hurry to reach the bow and our own fog-horn.

'Which way do you think it's going, Number One?'

He didn't answer straight away, but waited until the next long blast was borne muffled to us through the fog.

'You'd better let rip with that thing,' he said. 'I think it's coming our way.'

Our own fog-horn sounded timid and thin in comparison to the one we had just heard. I stabbed the button every ten seconds or so and tried not to think what would happen to us if we were run down. We'll probably never know if anyone aboard heard us, but I'm certain the ship never changed direction. It must have passed within a few hundred·yards of us, but we did not see a thing.

For a full half minute after it went by 'Rosie' was thrown violently about like some child's plaything in the wake, while John and I faced one another across the stern seat hardly daring to breathe. Finally the boat steadied and we both relaxed.

'By the time this trip is over,' I told John, 'I'm going to have white hair and a permanent nervous twitch. This is supposed to be summer and so far all we've had is gales and fog. You could swear we were back in England.'

'I wish we were,' he said seriously. 'Then you could get out and go and ask a policeman where we are.'

Suddenly we both burst out laughing. It was not really a very funny joke, but if I hadn't found relief in laughter I think I would have exploded. Nervous tension had been building up—as it always did—during the storm. But now, as the danger was passing, one of us managed to say something to ease the pressure. It was something that happened often.

At last there was no more laughter left in us and we began to sing. We unshipped the oars and, bawling 'Rule Britannia' at the top of our voices, settled down once more to rowing. For eleven hours, with only a half-hour break for lunch, we pulled hard, knowing that every stroke brought the big dory closer towards England and home.

By midday the fog had dispersed completely. The sun was almost directly overhead and soon wisps of steam were rising from our damp clothes.

This was our second really long spell on the oars and I found at the end of it that my hands were beginning to swell. John held out his hands, palm upwards, and I saw a line of callouses beginning to form along his fingers. The sides of his knuckles were also swollen.

'And on top of that I've got another blister forming down here,' he said, patting his backside. 'It's being rubbed raw on that seat.'

Before we started our trip John had always maintained that it was pointless to practise the actual rowing of our boat. It was advice that I had willingly accepted, and apart from the two hours spent carrying out tests in the Solent, we had left the oars strictly alone.

My own experience was limited to the half hour which I had passed with Maureen rowing a small boat on the Serpentine in London's Hyde Park. By this time I was beginning to appreciate that hauling a ton and a half craft across the Atlantic was a far cry from messing about in a five-bob-an-hour fifteen-footer.

By the end of that day my back was aching badly and my arms felt as though they were being torn from their sockets. If I had been back in my local betting shop at Hawick, and anyone had been fool enough to give me odds of a hundred to one, I would not have risked my money on being able to complete the three thousand miles that still lay between us and the English coast.

It was also, in those early days, that the pattern began to emerge which was to govern our day-to-day life in the weeks ahead. On the fourth day out John introduced a ploy which was eventually to develop into a standing joke between us. For a reason best known to himself John never wanted to make the actual suggestion that we stop rowing.

'Do you think it's time we had a meal?' he said.

'I'm not fussy,' I replied.

He was silent for a few moments.

'I suppose we ought to try sorting out the provisions. What do you think?'

'They are in a bit of a mess, but I don't see that it will hurt to leave them a little longer.'

He considered this for the time it took to row half a dozen strokes. Then:

'How are your hands? Shall we stop and put some more lanoline on?'

'Mine are all right. But if you want to stop, then go ahead.'

'Oh for God's sake, Chay, don't you think we've done enough rowing for one bloody day?'

I grinned.

'Well, if you put it like that, yes.'

'You ought to have been a general,' he laughed, hauling in the long oars. 'You're too damned tricky for me by half.'

I am glad we stopped when we did, for if we hadn't I think I would have crumpled where I sat. Every muscle in my body was crying out for a rest. The strain of the previous three days had taken a lot out of me and all I wanted at that moment was to stretch out on the floor-boards and go to sleep. But I was determined that John should not know it. I deliberately rowed on two or three more strokes after he had stopped, and then casually hauled in my oars.

'Sure you don't want to go on for a while?' I asked innocently.

'I'm damned certain of it. But if you want to go on I suppose I better had too.'

I pretended to consider this for a few seconds.

'Well, there is a long way to go, so we'd better not overdo it.'

His face flooded with relief, and he quickly reached for the spare sea anchor. With practised fingers he lashed the line to our stem post and threw the thing over the side. When the rocking slowed to a barely noticeable roll I set to work reorganising our provisions, by this time spread in wild disorder along the full length of the boat.

It took half an hour to restow everything to our satisfaction. Then we quickly peeled off our clothes and were soon stretched out basking in the warm sun. The movement of the boat and the soothing effect of the sun's heat on my body did much to dispel the fears I still harboured about our progress.

'The Gulf Stream can't be very far away now,' I said. 'All we've got to do is row like mad for the next couple of days and we'll be there.'

John was half asleep. 'I think you're being very optimistic if you think we'll make it in two days,' he murmured. 'But you're right about one thing—we're going to have to row ourselves silly to stand any chance of making it at all.'

As I tucked my blanket all around me I quickly drifted into an untroubled sleep. I determined to redouble my own efforts on the oars the following day and make sure John did the same.

For the first time the weather seemed to be on our side. We slept late and the sun was already high in a cloudless blue sky when we took our seats, dry and re-freshed, to eat breakfast. The uninterrupted sleep had strengthened our resolve to make this the 'big effort' day. John made quite a speech about the loss of face our being driven ashore would cause to ourselves, the regi-ment and our families.

'I fully agree with you,' I told him. 'So let's waste no more time talking and get stuck in.'

We rowed for twelve hours, almost non-stop, the only real break being the hour we took for lunch. For most of that day I wore nothing more than a pair of pants, and these only to protect my backside from the seat.

During the afternoon we attracted the attention of a passing school of porpoises. They seemed fascinated by our boat and circled, dived and leapt around us for several hours. How much simpler it would be, I thought, if we could get them to lead us to the Gulf Stream. But we appeared to be making good progress. Even our failure to attract the attention of a flying boat and a distant merchant ship did not dampen our spirits.

By nightfall we came to within a mile of a group of trawlers, which we assumed to be the Russian fishing fleet off Georges Bank. Then, to our bitter disappoint-ment, we began to drift back the way we had come. There was nothing we could do to hold our position. The wind had turned, and it was a waste of effort to try to row against it.

That night we slept in two-hour shifts, practising the system we intended to adopt, when and if we ever reached the Gulf Stream. Had we known what was in store for us on the following day, we would have aban-doned the shift system and taken what sleep we could.

Very early in the morning I was woken out of a gale-haunted sleep by an agitated cry from John, 'Get up. We're about to be hit by a thunderstorm.'

I was suddenly aware of snaking tongues of lightning

lancing down out of the sky behind us. These were followed almost immediately by a long low growl of thunder.

In the thin pre-dawn light I could see the heavy seas building up, and as I scrambled to my seat a sudden rush of water over the side soaked me from the waist down.

The waves were like huge sand dunes that grew taller and more rounded as I watched. By the time I had taken my first long, arm-wrenching pull on the oars the lightning was crackling almost overhead.

The forking tongues seemed to dive down in every direction and I feared that being the only object for miles around we stood a good chance of being struck. Fortunately there was little rain and the storm soon passed away from us, pushed rapidly to the north-east by the rising wind.

Then the fog came rolling towards us in great swirling banks from the south-west, and by full daylight visibility was down to under fifty yards.

We agreed to keep rowing for as long as we appeared to be making any sort of headway, but by ten o'clock the waves on all sides had risen to more than twenty feet and further rowing became impossible.

As John slid his oars inboard he let go of one of them for a moment. It was snatched instantly away by the hungry sea and swirled out of sight into the fog.

I craned my neck over the side and shouted against the wind, 'Did you see how quickly that went?' John nodded.

'Do you think we'd go as fast as that if one of us went over the side?' I yelled. He nodded again, and I thought it time we tightened our safety harnesses. In gales such as this there was a strong possibility that our boat might be capsized. There were handles fixed to the underside, and we had practised righting her while testing in the

Solent. But I had little doubt that if our fingers slipped loose, for even a second, we might be drowned.

While all this was running through my head John was trying to coax a small bird into the boat. It was a yellow landbird which must have got lost in the fog. As it circled us it dipped lower and lower towards the water and was obviously at the end of its tether. I whistled, and John held out scraps of food, but it would not land, and eventually it flew away, making desperate efforts to maintain its height while dropping lower all the time. It upset us both to think that the bird would probably be dead within a few minutes.

We spent most of that night crouched over the pumps, as wave after wave broke over the side, filling the cockpit almost to seat level. Again we were carried to within a mile of the Russian fishing boats. We hoped we might reach them so that we could tie up to one and have the benefit of its anchor until the gale had blown itself out.

The wind blew us past, well to the north of them, and we never came closer than a mile to the nearest boat. John insisted that it was much too dangerous to pull the canvas canopy over its frame, so we spent the night out in the open, huddled together for warmth. Dawn found us soaked and freezing cold, still at the pumps. Then, as the wind shifted round to the north-west, we began to make better headway.

We used the boat as a surf board all day and were driven rapidly towards the south-east and our rendezvous with the Gulf Stream. Conversation between us was difficult as, with the noise of the wind and the water, we had to shout at the tops of our voices to be heard at all. By midnight we were too exhausted to keep awake any longer, and so, placing our lives and the safety of our boat in the hands of God, we crept under the canvas hood and fell into a troubled sleep.

By the morning the wind had changed yet again. But still it was not in our favour. It had shifted to the southeast, and to stop ourselves being pushed back towards land we unshipped our sea anchor and hove to for the next twenty-four hours.

It was not until after breakfast that we realised that today was a Sunday. Sunday, June 12. We stopped rowing. Neither of us said anything. I repeated the Lord's Prayer to myself. Afterwards John told me he did the same. It took only a few minutes, then we picked up the oars again.

I wanted to say something myself, but didn't know how to put it. Then I caught sight of the words of prayer engraved on the plaque, screwed to the hull.

'Oh God, thy sea is so great and my boat is so small,' I read. 'For the sake of our wives and ourselves please use one to spare the other.'

There was a tendency for us both to drop asleep whenever we were not rowing; and on a day like this, when rowing was out of the question, it would have been simple to sleep right through.

This, we decided, would be bad for morale. So we wrote down a list of chores to keep us occupied. One piece of equipment requiring urgent attention was the little French gas cooker. Both the one we were using, and the spare, were corroding fast. John spent most of the day cleaning them and coating the parts with a thick layer of vaseline.

My own task that Sunday was to check through all our rations. We had taken on enough tins, fresh fruit, vegetables and groceries to last us about a week. And so far we had not needed to break into our rations proper. The plan had been partially successful. Out of the two dozen eggs we bought we had eaten fifteen and the rest were broken in the storms. Some of the fruit and vegetables had gone rotten: I threw them over the side. But I

47

found there were enough American-bought stores intact to keep us going for another two days.

This, at least, was heartening news.

'All we have to do now,' John said, when I told him, 'is to find a more comfortable way of sleeping, and it will be like living in a holiday camp.'

That was when he presented the Ridgway solution to the 'kipping problem'.

'Instead of doubling up between the sides we must raise our beds to the level of the thwarts, and we will be able to lie straight out,' he explained.

'If we tie ourselves down it won't matter if our feet hang over the edge a bit.'

I was very doubtful if his plan would work, but nothing, I thought, could be worse than the sleeping positions we were already using.

I was wrong.

We piled some of the plastic water bags at either end and used the life rafts to raise the platforms to the height of the thwarts.

'Okay,' said John, 'let's give 'em a try.'

They were terrible—very hard and very uncomfortable—and we rocked in an alarming fashion as the water bags slid about below. I tried for an hour to sleep—and then gave it up. When I looked round I saw John was sitting on his rowing seat, head in hands. He glanced up and our eyes met.

'Do you have any more bright ideas?' I asked. John grinned.

'Yes. Let's get these damned life rafts and water bags stowed away and turn in for some sleep.'

Hurricane Alma

John Ridgway: June 13–21

I MAY not be a Master Mariner, but I had covered many thousands of miles of sea before the day that Chay and I set out in *English Rose III*. I had studied navigation, sailed with the Merchant Navy and spent many happy hours in small boats, so I knew something about life at sea and the strange wonderment that comes over you when you feel at one with the ocean. I knew the glories of the brilliant sunrises and sunsets when the whole of the sea seems to be a moving flood of reds and golds and purples.

I had found peace at sea before. I had also found that you have to be an exceptionally strong man to be a seaman. I do not mean a great, tough thug of a person. But you have to be a complete person—mature, sensible and responsible if you are going to consider any type of voyage over the great oceans of the world.

You also have to realise—for the very breadth and hugeness of the sea forces this upon you—that you must be humble. There can be no flouting the sea. Foolhardy gestures, flamboyance, bravado lead to your undoing. Relax your guard for one second and the sea will have you.

Certainly the North Atlantic is a cruel sea, and with every day that passed we both came to realise the truth of this. But it has its wonders and delights. Some of these I had seen before and they had been half-forgotten and left lying in some small, tucked-away portion of my memory.

Chay had seen nothing before. At the beginning there was almost incredulous disbelief on his face as the ocean opened before him. The flicker of the sun through fly-ing spume, the lift of the bow of the boat rising to the never-ending succession of waves, the gurgle of water rippling along the sides of the boat and the grace and freedom of the seagulls as they swooped and circled a few feet from our heads—all these things were some small miracle to Chay.

I shall never forget the look on his face when he saw his first whale. I had seen whales before, but this first sighting of the enormous mammal from a small boat which was only inches off the sea certainly had me worried for a moment or two.

'Chay, do you see that—a whale?' and I pointed over the sea towards the back of the monster, which looked like a small, barren island that the sea had just regurgi-tated.

It was not the biggest whale in the seas, but I sud-denly realised what this must look like to Chay, who, after all, had rarely seen anything bigger than a large salmon. It was the look on his face that told me what he was thinking as it seemed to amble through the water towards us with an idle flick of its mammoth tail.

'God,' Chay said—and it was a prayer, not an ex-clamation. 'What a size—just look at the jet it's blown out. That's it breathing, I suppose.'

It spouted again and the wind caught the water and sprayed it close by. There was an odd smell, a deep fishy smell similar to that you might find on a summer's day walking down Billingsgate Market. It really was huge. We seemed to peer up at it as though at the side of a passing double-decker bus.

Suddenly the great head of the giant turned. It was

pointing straight at us and came towards us slowly, in-exorably. It was menacing, and I do not care who knows it, I was frightened. Only feet away from the side of 'Rosie' it dived—not the lightsome, frolicking dive of a porpoise or a dolphin, but the steady, sinking, rumbling dive of a submarine. It passed right under the boat, and I felt 'Rosie' stir and shiver from the disturbed water set up by the whale.

'We'll be lost, look out!' cried Chay.

He dived too—for his safety harness—and buckled it on quickly.

'That thing will overturn us and everything will be lost. Hang on, John!' Chay shouted.

I can understand his anxiety—he had never seen a whale that close before. But neither had I, and I was feeling exactly the same. But if we were going to be overturned, then we were going to be overturned and there was nothing we could do about it. So I sat tight and waited.

After a minute or two nothing happened. I looked at Chay and he looked back. I am sure the exchange of looks would be very similar to that swopped by a couple of elderly spinsters who had seen a mouse run under their chair a minute earlier and were waiting for the first touch of a twitching nose on their ankles. Another minute passed. Then we just grinned. The whale must have gone.

'I don't want many more shocks like that,' Chay said. I agreed. It had been frightening. But it was memor-able. There are not all that number of people in the world who have seen a whale at such close quarters while they were voyaging in a tiny boat far from land. I will not forget it, neither the fear of it nor the wonder. And I know Chay will not, either. It was an incident, too, which took our minds off the greater terrors—the sea itself and the enormity of our task.

The sea was not something you could forget for long. Although Chay and I had a yarn about whales and their habits and their extraordinary powers which enabled them to swim thousands of miles and navigate as expertly to a landfall as the Captain of the *Queen Mary,* the sea soon intruded once again into our thoughts.

I remembered the horror of Hurricane Alma. I knew about hurricanes—in theory. I knew the power of the winds at their centres could reach more than 120 m.p.h., that ships had disappeared in them never to be heard of again. I knew, too, that the winds built up mountains of water with breaking peaks that weighed hundreds of tons.

I knew, too, that there were sudden shifts of wind which brought seas from a completely different direction in a very short time indeed. I shuddered when I read of the cross seas that could run at the height of a hurricane. Seamen who had experienced them said that it was like two mountains approaching each other at the speed of a racehorse and crashing together. I thought that if we were ever caught in a hurricane it would be the end for 'Rosie' and ourselves.

I had also remembered reading as a boy some of the great stories of disaster at sea caused by hurricane or tornado or just a plain, straightforward gale.

As a soldier I had obviously been interested in the other two Services, the Royal Navy and the Royal Air Force, and had studied the problems that they faced. I had read of ships in the last war which were caught in North Atlantic hurricanes. These were horror stories of guns and boats being carried away, of breaking seas ripping armour-plated tops off turrets, of bridges being crushed and their occupants crushed to death or swept into the wild waters like leaves in an autumn breeze.

So it was with some concern that I heard a radio

broadcast at 12.20 p.m. on June 13. The announcer interrupted a programme—I cannot recall what—and read a brief message. 'Hurricane Alma is due off Cape Cod this evening and is expected to turn north-east-wards.' Turn, in other words, right at us.

I was astonished by this report as well as alarmed. It was, of course, a reassuring message for those on shore, and I was relieved that our many friends back in Orleans would not have to suffer the havoc of Alma. But I was astonished—for Alma was too soon. The hurricane season was August and September—at least that was what I had been taught. And then I remembered that in some years, perhaps ten or fifteen years apart, the hurricane season began early.

It looked as though hurricanes were a little early this year.

I told Chay what I had heard and said that we could expect Alma to arrive in a few hours' time. But he had heard the message as well, and his face showed me that he was as worried as I was.

'What do we do now?' Chay said.

I knew that my limited experience would be tested to the full and that any sea lore I had picked up on my way through life must be remembered, for our lives would depend on my memory. I explained to Chay what we must expect and did not pull any punches when I talked about the dangers of hurricanes. Chay was not too surprised, I suppose because the very word 'hurricane' conjures up to an alert and imaginative man the perils of the sea.

'Well, Chay, we must make everything ready. We must think ahead so that when the seas and the winds are high we don't have to risk our lives trying to secure things in the boat,' I told him. 'We must put the sea anchor out as soon as the first winds start up so that we are not blown back to the Cape if the wind comes from the East.'

It was by now a pleasant day, a little misty, with lots of birds about. The boat looked fine, still freshly painted with everything in good shape. So I decided to take some ciné and still photographs with our cameras.

I saw Chay looking at me a little anxiously, but I thought this was because he was still worrying about the broadcast. He put me right in a moment. 'What on earth are you up to, John? Don't you realise we might be dead in a few hours, that we've got work to do if we're to try and stay alive. And yet all you do is take pictures as though you were a Francis Drake playing bowls. Let's get moving.'

I could see his point, all right, but I was not playing this thing cool. I had not meant to seem like Drake. What I needed was time. Time to think and scrape that memory of mine for sea lore, and taking pictures was a good way of gaining time.

I have got this approach to life which some people mistake for courage. I do not make this a conscious effort to impress—it just happens. It is like this. I think of everything that can go wrong—or, at least, I try to—and then work out how to answer the challenge. Once I have made out the list of 'things to do', that is that. I say to myself, 'John, you've thought of everything and done everything you can to ensure your safety. There's nothing more you can do except sit.' So I sit. People think I am brave. In fact, it is a form of laziness.

So I took Chay's point and we did get cracking. We lashed everything so that if we should be capsized we would not lose any kit or be hit by a heavy piece of equipment.

We prepared our sea anchor ready to stream it and we had some food. If we were to be hit by Alma at least we would have a good meal inside us.

But even though we were dreading the night before us, we realised that we must press on as best we could towards our goal. So when Chay and I had made all our preparations we decided to row just a bit more that day. Out came the oars again and we rowed and yarned trying to hide our apprehension by talking about the past.

At 8 p.m. we felt the first breath of wind. Soon there was a stiff breeze, although there was still some mist about. Chay suggested we called it a day and got some sleep before Alma caught up with us. He quite rightly said that we might not be able to sleep for a long time and that our physical reserves would be strengthened by sleep. We got the tarpaulin out, snuggled as best we could into our uncomfortable beds with their mattresses of life rafts and water bags and prepared for the worst.

I could not drop off that night. I lay on the bottom of the boat listening to the water swirling round the boat and nervously heard the wind freshen and the seas begin to increase. The seas were not strong nor the wind high—we were to go through far worse—but it was my wretched imagination at work. I could not get out of my mind those stories of storms at sea and I could see in my half-sleep those men being plucked off their wartime ships and cast into the ocean. But in the end I slept.

We slept for nearly twelve hours, a dreamless night so far as I can remember now. We were both awoken at the same moment by Hurricane Alma and hundreds of gallons of swirling, grey Atlantic water which crashed on to our backs and half filled 'Rosie'. One moment asleep, the next fighting for our lives. I can never remember waking up so swiftly or so completely before. The scene on that roaring frightening morning was awful.

The wind was screaming, whipping the tops off thirty-foot-high waves and flinging them more violently than any rainstorm straight into our eyes. We could only see by half turning our backs and screwing up our eyes to keep out the slashing, stinging salt water.

'Rosie' was alive, the sort of aliveness that you might find in a demented animal crazed by the nearness of death. She was bucketing, pitching and rolling in the seas despite the enormous amount of water swilling inside her. For a moment I seemed completely detached as though I was sitting in the front row of the stalls at a London theatre on a first night. I saw our beds were under water. I noticed that Chay's face was green with the stain from the tarpaulin cover. It was a mad world, a world made up of punishing noise, violent movement. I suppose I took all this in within a few moments, but I shall always remember the sheer terror of that Atlantic awakening to Alma.

Chay and I screamed at each other over the roar. 'Bail, for God's sake bail.'

We grabbed a bucket each and bailed. We did not seem to be gaining on the water, for as soon as we threw ten bucketfuls out another ten would come inboard, either from the breaking seas as we were rocketed like maniacs on a watery switchback or from the driving white spume.

As we battled I remembered saying to myself: 'Thank God for that training, those daily runs. Thank God I'm fit. I could never face this if I was a soft, white-collar worker.' So we bailed. I don't know for how long —it seemed like years—and gradually we got that water in the boat under control.

We both then huddled down as best we could to rest. Our lungs were gasping for air from the enormous exertion we had put into our fight for life. After a few minutes we were able to look at each other and raise a kind of smile of encouragement to each other. I know Chay's grin, not quite as carefree as it normally is, bucked me up a lot.

So I started to think again. I realised that 'Rosie' was not a dying boat. Certainly she was still being thrown around, but she was riding well. I had a sudden surge of affection for those phlegmatic Northerners from Bradford who had built her. She was all right, a great boat.

I did a quick check of our gear. Everything was still lashed. We did not appear to have lost a thing. It just shows that you must look ahead when you are on the ocean. If we had left the job of lashing until the weather got bad we would have lost a large proportion of our vital gear.

What of ourselves? I asked Chay if he was all right. 'You must be joking,' he shouted back. 'I'm drenched through, I'm cold, I'm hungry and I'm frightened to death. It's all right for you, you're used to mucking about in small boats. I'm not. I suppose I'm okay. I'm alive and no bones broken.'

We had to get organised again. We could not relax, for the wind still continued to scream and the water still came inboard and I saw that while we had taken our breather the bottom boards were already awash again.

So we decided that one would use the pumps, which were capable of getting rid of eight gallons of water a minute, while the other rested as best he could under the tarpaulin. There was no hope of getting dried out or of changing into dry clothes. But at least the tarpaulin would keep the chill off and give the man resting a chance to regain his strength. Looking back, it was a miserable, depressing way to have a rest. But at the time it seemed like heaven to snuggle up under the tarpaulin out of the wind and wet.

I took the first stint on the pump while Chay went under cover. He even managed to sleep, for I saw his eyes close and his regular, undisturbed breathing. He looked rather like a young boy asleep on that chaotic morning. I did not have much time for brotherly thoughts, however, as there was a job to be done. I grabbed the pump handle and pumped. Each time the boat lurched I seemed to be thrown against a sharp projection on our equipment. But the pumping had to go on. It was agonising. The strain was on my arm and the monotony of pump, pump and pump, pump, was enough to drive one stupid.

But I kept at it, for I knew that this was not the moment to give up. One piece of relaxation and we might be lost, for I kept thinking over and over again that the cruel sea would only strike if you gave it a chance. So pump, pump and pump, pump.

At the end of half an hour I woke Chay and he took over the pump and I tucked myself up in the tarpaulin. I could not understand how I could feel so cold on a June morning, but I was shivering, worn out and glad to get under cover.

However, I found that although there was some comfort being out of the spray and wind, another discomfort crept in. I suddenly felt seasick. I had been sick early in the voyage, a thing that I had half expected to happen. I should have got used to 'Rosie's' movement by now. I had not—and I felt very sick. Part of it was anxiety, I suppose, part the astonishing gyrations of our tiny boat, which seemed to do everything except loop the loop or capsize.

So it was agony for me to struggle out from under the canvas to relieve Chay. He looked old now, strained and anxious. I suppose I must have looked the same. We did not look like soldiers from the Parachute Regiment. We looked like old tramps who had spent a week under old newspapers in the pouring rain in a draughty corner of a Midland slum. We certainly looked horrible.

And so it went on until noon. The wind did not abate and it was still causing heavy seas and the spume was still flying and we were still screwing our eyes up as a shield against the salt spray.

I was frightened all the time and so was Chay. 'I'm plain worried,' he told me. 'Why do I do these things? I've had nine years in the Army and I should've learned by now that you never volunteer for nothing "not nohow".'

Both of us prayed. As I worked at the pump I would pray for help and guidance. I felt that I was responsible for 'Rosie' and Chay. I had asked him to come with me and I knew that he trusted in my seamanship and navigation. So I prayed that God might aid me in my task to save us from Hurricane Alma.

Chay prayed as well. I would see his lips moving as he laid down in the boat. I knew he had seen me pray. There was no feeling of self-consciousness—we knew that we were right to pray.

I was pumping one moment and I caught a movement out of the corner of my eye, a tiny flash of white. I screwed my eyes up and peered closely to where I had seen this on the swirling water close to the boat, and I saw an astonishing sight. For there, tucked up close in the lee of *English Rose III* were a dozen or so sea-birds. I thought of the hundreds of birds there must be over the ocean and wondered what happened to them when a screaming hurricane hit an area. Did they drown, were they smashed in the seas? I was happy to know that a dozen of them would be alive because of us. It was good to know that 'Rosie' was saving us and the birds.

I watched them; their feathers ruffled when an eddy of wind caught them. They were really close to the boat, only feet away. As 'Rosie' rolled I thought that they must be crushed by the gunwales, but each time they seemed to sense the danger and just paddle an inch or two to get clear. It was fascinating to watch them, and doing so prevented me thinking quite so much about our own peril.

I changed places with Chay again. He was in better shape than I was, and I think that this was because I picked a bad position to pump from. I kept getting drenched and water was running constantly through my clothes and down my body. As the water temperature was only 48 degrees Fahrenheit it did not take much of this to make you feel you were sitting in an icebox. I think that I was on the verge of suffering from exposure, and looking back, that coldness and exhaustion was probably the cause of my seasickness.

That morning seemed unending. The seas showed no sign of abating and the wind still roared. The spume and spray that lashed us seemed to be as vicious and as determined as birds of prey—they tore and worried and harried us.

I was dozing at about lunchtime when Chay shouted at me and I stirred, but did not make any real effort to answer him. I was more or less comfortable and it took too much energy even to say, 'Yes.'

Then I was wide awake again. I had heard Chay shout my name and he was a good six feet away. Up to then we had had to put our heads almost together and shout to be heard above the noise of Alma. But here I was hearing him quite clearly. The noise had decreased.

'John, wake up. I think we're through it. I think we'll live. We've made it,' came Chay's shouts. His eyes were laughing.

So we were through it. We had beaten a hurricane in a twenty-foot open boat. The seas were still high and the wind was still blowing hard; but it was no worse than an earlier gale. We were through the worst.

It was an uncomfortable afternoon, as we were still wet and aching in every limb from fighting the crazy movements of 'Rosie'. We were bruised too, from the constant bumps against the sharp edges in the boat. Morale began to suffer as well after an hour or two, and we both longed to be out of that wearying, miserable, never-ending motion and on land again.

Chay had the idea that finally got us back to a proper mental state.

'John, how about some grub? We should be able to get the stove going. A hot meal, curry and rice and a cup of cocoa, how about it?' he asked.

Of course it was the answer. Chay set to. How he managed in that violent motion I do not know. He dragged our cooking utensil out; at that time it was a shiny new, aluminium pressure cooker. He broke into the first of our full ration packs, found the curry—a dehydrated bar containing meat and sultanas and looking like a large crumbly Oxo cube—and the packet of rice that went with it.

Then out came the water which he poured over the concoction in the bottom of the pan. He got the stove going and suddenly there was that smell. I can recall it now, the rich, spicy smell of curry. I lay there sniffing. It was then I realised how hungry I was; my mouth watered and I became more and more impatient.

Chay handed the pan to me at last with our one and only spoon, a long-handled wooden thing. I gulped the first two or three mouthfuls and food had never tasted better. I could feel it going right down. I was alive again and feeling warm. I stopped when I had eaten half, which was about half a pound of solid grub. I handed the pan over to Chay and I watched him wolf his portion. Every mouthful he took was an agony because I could have eaten four helpings and still have felt hungry.

But Chay had not finished with the meal yet. 'I've got a sweet, John, just to round the day off,' and he gave me a bar of rum fudge. My goodness, how delicious that was.

And so Hurricane Alma went her way and we ours. We were left alive and with the thought that nothing worse than that June 14 could come along.

We slept and awoke to fog and a ship. It was the trawler *Winchester,* who stopped, and her skipper and crew chatted with us. It was good to hear new voices, but the news they gave us was bad. We found that after twelve days at sea we had only covered 120 miles—ten miles a day. That was really bad.

We had been blown back for the third time to the Georges Bank. It was the hurricane and the easterly winds that had stopped our progress, and we were both thoroughly depressed. One of the crew shouted down that the trawler was going to Boston, Massachusetts. 'Why don't you give up now, Mac, pack it in? It's much too far to row. Use your heads.'

For a fraction of a second I was tempted. Dry clothes, a good meal, sleep and the stillness of land—what a prospect. But it was only for a fraction, and both Chay and I shouted back, 'No thanks. It's good of you to offer us a lift, but we'll press on.'

When she slipped away into the mist of the fishing grounds Chay and I had a good long, down-to-earth talk. We decided that we had been messing about too much, not spending enough time at the oars. We had somewhere lost the drive that we needed to conquer the Atlantic.

So we worked out a routine. Both of us would row from eight each morning until half an hour before last light. One would make the grub and eat and switch round when the other fellow's turn came up. That would mean that the boat would always be driven through the water. At night we would row separately, two hours' sleep, two hours' row and so on.

I felt encouraged by this decision. We had our drive back. We were in top gear again. But the weeks to come were going to strain us and our rigid ideas. At this time we did not know that, which was probably a good thing.

I must say that when I thought about this voyage back in my home with my wife and my friends in the Regiment, I thought that there would be a dreary, dreadful monotony about life and that time would hang heavy. But I began to find that there was never enough time to keep the boat and the equipment in good order. And there was always something happening on those broad waters.

June 16 was a sunny day, a clear blue sky and the water was flat calm—what a difference. We started to row a bit later than we had planned, at about 10 a.m., mainly because we had rowed until nearly midnight the night before.

At eleven-thirty we saw a large ship about four or five miles away, but we did not make any signals to her. She just kept on her way, serene, imperturbable. A little while later I had a look for some rations out of the polystyrene box that Chay had opened the night before for our curry. I found that part of the week's rations were damaged and uneatable—soaked in salt water despite all the protective coverings.

I felt a bit anxious at this and checked some more of the unopened boxes. Some of these had been ruined. That was obviously Alma's doing—we had not got away scotfree as we had both thought. We talked this over and thought that we might have to reduce our rations later on. Even then we had not realised the damage that Alma had left in her wake.

We rowed some more after I had made lunch from a dehydrated fish bar brought almost to life again by boiling in water. In fact, it was pretty horrid and mushy. But it was food. Later on we were to long for these mushes when food got short.

In the afternoon the wind got up again, but we kept

on rowing until seven-thirty when we had dinner—
curry again! And so to sleep. That day, a quiet one for
us, had kept me full of interest from the time I awoke
until the time came for me to get under the tarpaulin
and go to sleep. There was never enough time.

During the next few days we had fogs and mists, we
saw porpoises and whales—one which seemed like a
travelling Nissen hut, it was so huge. It was worrying
being in the fog, as we heard sirens and once or twice
the rush of a ship travelling fast through the water not
far from us. I had doubts about our position again—
surely we were not back once more among the fishing
fleet on the Georges Bank—and I felt rather depressed
about our progress. But June 19 was to cheer me up considerably, for we saw a ship and I found my estimated
position was very nearly spot on with the position she
gave us.

We saw four ships close together at about 10 a.m. and
one saw us and came towards us. Chay thought it was a
fishing factory ship first of all, as there was a smaller
vessel close by, and he thought she was transferring her
catch.

The ship turned out to be the *Albatross IV*, an oceanographic vessel from Woods Hole. They asked if we
needed anything, but I refused everything they offered
—we had wanted to be independent of anyone on the
ocean. But I changed my mind when I remembered that
our torches were out of action, so we took two torches
and spare batteries which they kindly offered us. We had
a general chat about weather, ocean currents and the
position which had so delighted me. She then rang on,
there was a tinkle of telegraphs deep below and a swirl
from her stern and she was gone.

We knew at least from the *Albatross* that the course
we had set was right and that we were heading correctly
towards the Gulf Stream with its warmer waters, its bril-

liant blue and the gentle drift which would help us on our way. It was a very satisfying morning.

Better than this, though, was their intention to report our position to Lloyd's of London. It would mean that our wives would know in a short time that we had survived Alma and that one of their worries was behind them.

We ran into another gale the next day and I was impressed by the way Chay managed to get to sleep during it. We had put the sea anchor out and got together under cover of the tarpaulin. I could not close my eyes and hung on in terror as the water and spray hit the tarpaulin and sloshed its way into the boat. I can only think that he was more tired than I was and just could not keep awake—but that would be strange for my tough comrade, who, I feel, has greater physical strength than I have.

Later the wind dropped, and all was well and we progressed gradually to the longest day, June 21, through a series of uneventful hours disturbed only by seeing sharks galore.

We managed to get a good sunbathe in the afternoon, rowing in really excellent weather. As I rowed I looked at my body and at Chay's as we took our steady pull at the oars in the nude. I was looking for damage, bruises, cuts, abrasions. We looked fine. To date we were unscarred by the Atlantic. It was a situation we knew could change—suddenly!

Sun and sharks

Chay Blyth: June 22–30

ALTHOUGH I had never been to sea before in my life, I think I can honestly say that by the time we had been out three weeks I was almost as good at the game as John. Of course, I still knew nothing about the fundamentals of seamanship and my knowledge of navigation was elementary—although I felt fairly certain that if it ever came to it I would be able to make my way alone.

But even a dyed-in-the-wool landlubber like myself could not fail to fall in with the swing of things, and after a few weeks I began to feel an extraordinary sense of oneness with the sea and all that was happening to us. Before we started, the prospect of going through a gale terrified the life out of me. As for a hurricane—I thought that would be like the end of the world. But we had been through gales and already we had experienced our first hurricane—and we had come through unscathed.

That does not mean to say that I had become blasé about the whole thing, that I was thinking of it as a holiday. It was far from that. I did not forget for one second that we were fighting against the elements and that we would have to drop our guard only once to receive the knock-out blow.

I was terrified at the prospect of falling overboard and being eaten by sharks. We had seen plenty of these enormous creatures; they seemed almost as long as my back garden at home. They were so close to the boat that

I could see their wicked-looking eyes, and their mouths were so big that I felt they could have swallowed both John and me together.

We had several brushes with these evil-looking creatures, and all the time I was weighing up this fear of them against my desire to go for a swim. I am a fair swimmer and love the water, and with the sun shining it was so hot rowing that the first thing I wanted to do was to strip off and dive in for a cooler. John kept telling me that swimming out there in water a couple of miles deep would seem a lot different from a dip in the local pool at Aldershot.

However, on Wednesday, June 22, it was so hot—John said he felt like Lawrence of Arabia in the desert—that the sea became more tempting than ever. We were wearing our white hats for the first time as protection from sunstroke, but the heat was taking its toll from us in energy. At two o'clock we had a break and I managed to fall asleep. At three we hove to and got all the tins of food from the stern and a change of clothes from the bow—a complicated but very necessary chore. Most of the clothing was still dry, but some biscuits and foot powder were a write-off as they had become sodden with the wet.

After this chore we felt too exhausted to row for a bit, and I suddenly announced, 'This heat is taking it out of me. Let's go in for a swim. It'll do us good.'

I was amazed when he agreed. The water looked so inviting; it was an iridescent blue with the sun shining full on it—just like one of those picture postcards you see for parts of the Mediterranean.

I watched enviously as John kicked off his Wellington boots, pulled off his trousers and underpants and threw his vest and jersey to the bottom of the boat.

'This is going to be good,' he said.

He stood up on the gunwales, his long blond hair

blowing in the breeze, and with a great grin on his stubbled face—we hadn't shaved for several days—he said, 'Here we go.'

But, instead of diving, John was apparently so exhilarated by the sun and the prospect of swimming that he decided to play the fool a little. This was strange behaviour for John, who tends to be somewhat more serious than me. Until now he had left the clowning to me.

I really did not like the idea of our going in for a dip because of the sharks. However, I thought the risk was worth taking because it was so hot and rowing for hours at a stretch under the sun was beginning to take it out of us.

John was in no hurry, but I was. I wanted John to get his cooler over with so that I could go in for a dip myself. I am afraid 'I showed my exasperation by telling him, 'If you don't hurry up, I'll damned well push you in.'

John took not the least bit of notice, so without another word I grabbed at both oars, placed the blades gently in the water and gave a hard tug. John lost his balance, flapped his arms madly for a moment, then fell forwards into the bottom of the boat.

Suddenly I felt an awful bitter taste in the back of my throat, and I was nearly sick, for as the boat moved a few yards further on from the spot where we had been resting, I spotted a black shape moving through the water. It was at least as long as the boat, and I watched paralysed as it cruised smoothly just below the surface and nudged its vicious-looking muzzle against the side of the boat.

We had seen so many odd creatures that I could not be absolutely certain that it was the most feared one of all—a shark. But there was no doubt about it, a second or two later. The fish glided to the surface, exposing above it a scimitar-like fin, similar to the weapon I had seen Arab tribesmen carry, when I was serving in the desert. At that moment an overwhelming sense of thankfulness went through me that John had delayed going for his swim. Had he not done so, he might have been eaten alive.

John clambered to his feet, rubbing a sore spot on his shins. 'That was a stupid thing to do,' he said. I did not reply, but continued to pull the boat round in a half circle so that we stood off about thirty yards from that evil-looking black dorsal fin which I could still see outlined against the sparkling blue water. I leaned back, pulled the oars inboard and told John to take a look.

He did not know what I was talking about.

'Take a look at that,' I said, pointing to the shark which by now had cruised silently to a point just forward of us.

John turned his head and gave a yelp of disbelief.

'My God,' he said. 'That was a near one.'

Normally John is what I would describe as a 'cool customer'. On this occasion it was different. He was quite clearly shocked by the thought of what might have happened if he had fallen out instead of into the boat.

It took him a good five minutes to recover. Meanwhile I decided that I would prepare something to eat and drink, a dehydrated fish bar and a cup of cocoa. As we were disposing of this in silence, both of us pondering on John's remarkable escape, he suddenly turned to me and said, 'I have always wanted to be in a tight spot where somebody would save my life. I must say that was quite an interesting experience. I shall never forget exactly how I felt when I saw that shark and realised I could have been in there with it. I felt so weak after you pointed it out that I thought I was going to faint.'

He thought for a moment and said, 'Just what would you have done if that shark had got me? I hope you would not have been quite silly enough to have dived in and tried to save me. If I had gone, do you think you could have managed the rest of the trip on your own?'

I thought for a moment and, finishing the last mouthful of my piece of fish that was tasting just like dry sawdust in my mouth, I replied, 'John—honestly I don't know what I would have done. But please take it easy in future.'

The whole of the area through which we were passing that day—June 22—must have been infested with sharks. The bright sunshine and good visibility enabled us to see quite a long way around us. Once we saw three of these enormous fish, each in its own territory, about half a mile apart. These sharks were very large, about twenty-five to thirty feet long.

John and I wondered why so many seemed to be swimming around 'Rosie' that day. We thought that it was the ripples through the water that we were making as we rowed gently onwards, and the noise of the oar-locks that attracted them.

But then John suddenly turned to me and said, 'You know what I think, Chay? I think that they know that this is the rubbish dump of the Atlantic and they are looking to snap up all sorts of odd little delicacies in this part of the ocean.'

This made sense, because all that day we had met a constant stream of debris scattered over the sea. There were half-empty tins, old electric-light bulbs, pieces of wood, even a child's beach ball—together with bits of old cabbage and even potato peelings. This is the sort of stuff that is thrown overboard by the kitchen staff of ocean liners at least three times a day. And in the middle of this uneatable mess there was the inevitable piece of meat or bone or offal which the shark could smell hundreds of yards away.

I noted in my log that day that we had seen at least five of these monsters, some close to the boat, others a distance away, and whenever we saw one it sent a shiver of fear through us both.

Just for a change we had a dreamless night despite the anxiety that we had both felt about the sharks. This was probably because the sea was calm and we were able to relax during our two-hour spells underneath the tarpaulin without being thrown from side to side by movement of 'Rosie' and without being awakened by the stream of salt water pouring down our necks.

We awoke early to another lovely day, and we were both rowing again by half past five in the morning.

John turned to me. 'Chay, now that we have got a calm patch we had better get the rations organised. Let's get all those packs and boxes stowed away properly, because some of them are still getting in the way when we are rowing at night.'

So I spent the next hour or so stacking the boxes. One of them I found had a broken lid, but I was not very worried, because I knew all the dehydrated bars of food were sealed in waterproof bags. Just to make sure that our food was still all right I opened up one of the boxes —one that we could have next week.

I found one of the fish bars was sopping wet, rather like shredded wheat that had been soaked in cold water, a really horrible soggy mess. I opened another box and yet another, and I went through about one-third of our rations with my back all the time turned to John, so that he could not see the panic of my movements and the fear in my face.

But I had to tell him. I had to tell him that from then on our rations of calories would be cut by one-third. John had asked me to study the calory and vitamin problems, and he had left it to me to arrange for supplies which would maintain us at a full peak of fitness.

'I have got some very bad news,' I told him. 'We have lost about a third of our rations. I don't know how this happened, but there is box after box absolutely soaked through. The rum is gone as well, so that means we will not be able to take a nip if things get bad or if we get cold. We must have stowed it badly when we set out.'

John turned and looked at me, and in a quite un-flustered way he said, 'Do you know what Field Marshal Slim said when our blokes in Burma seemed to be in really bad trouble?'

I wondered what the hell he was getting at. I thought he had lost track of where we were and what had happened.

I thought I'd humour him. So I said, 'No, John, I don't.'

' "Things are seldom as good or as bad as they are first reported." That's what he said.'

So I separated out box by box, dehydrated bar by bar, what we had lost.

John said, 'We should have made this check imme-diately after Hurricane Alma had died down. We must remember at all times—if we relax the sea will have us.'

If we had checked our food as soon as Alma died down we would have been laughing. Still, I suppose John was right and it could have been worse. When we made a check of the other damaged boxes the next day, taking turn about to go through a complete box, we found that the items most affected by the sea were the beef cubes and rice, the pepper (our only spice), the apple flakes, which we usually had for breakfast, and the soup. Other-wise the remaining supplies were not too badly damaged —except that our Spangles, Enerzades and Horlicks tablets were spoiled in the boxes which had had the lids broken.

Later that day John said that the back of his neck was feeling very sore and he could hardly turn his head for the pain. I told him to stop rowing and to bow his head

so that I could have a look to see if I could see anything
wrong.

I saw a great boil, a really bad one, inflamed round
the edges and with a great head looking like the top of a
volcano. I supposed this must be part of the poison
coming out from the poisoned leg of his which never
really got the chance to clear up before we sailed.

I said, 'You are in a very bad way, Number One. This
means an immediate operation. You have the nastiest
boil I have ever seen in all my first-aid days,' and I went
to the medical kit and produced scalpels, disinfectant,
needles and thread for making stitches.

'This is going to hurt you a great deal. You may lose
some blood. The water may have got in. I don't know
whether this thing is sterilised.'

He said, 'All right, Chay. Get it over with as quickly
as you can.'

I made him turn his back to me so he could not see
the medical kit, which I had placed on the thwart beside
me.

'Are you ready, John?'

'Yes.'

I took a soft lint bandage and placed it gently on top
of the boil and fastened it with two strips of plaster.

John sat, his head still bowed and a look of some
anxiety on his face, waiting for me—a very amateur doctor—to do my worst.

'That's it, you are all fixed up. You can relax now,' I
told him.

'That was marvellous, Chay. I did not feel a thing.
That medical training you were given before we left
really has helped.'

He turned round and saw me grinning all over my
face.

'What are you laughing at? I can tell you that having
a boil lanced is not a very pleasant thing,' John said.

73

I just could not stop laughing, and John got more and more annoyed with me the more I laughed, and in the end I had to own up.

'I am sorry, John, I know I should not have conned you like this, but it was all a big show—all I have done is put a dressing on. All the sawbones cutlery was for show.'

I thought for a moment John was going to thump me.

But then he laughed too and said, 'You great lout —you wait until you have got a boil. There won't be a soft dressing for you—only a blunt knife.'

Late that night a merchant ship passed us quite close. We could hear the hum of the generators and the thump of the diesels driving her through the water. We fired a mini-flare, not because we really needed anything but because we would like to have heard someone else's voice—anyone's voice, even if he was talking in a foreign tongue.

But the ship carried on its way. I was astonished. I could not understand how the vessel could pass us so close without seeing our flare, and I wondered if any of these ships kept a look-out on the bridge.

'Supposing we had been in trouble, John? Supposing we had fired our big rockets? Do you think they would have seen us then? What would happen if we were dying in the middle of the ocean—would they still pass by unheeding?'

John thought for a moment or two. 'Not to worry, Chay. Don't forget we have got our radio, and if they don't see the rockets they must hear our emergency radio call, because all these ships keep a round-the-clock watch on the radio distress frequency.' But as I settled down for my two hours of sleep I wondered if he was right.

Early next morning a tern decided to accompany us. One of these graceful Arctic-white birds would often circle the boat for hours, obviously regarding it as his personal floating larder.

Soon another tern dived to the challenge, and we watched the swooping, squawking, pecking aerial combat until the weaker bird retreated, leaving the victor, ever circling, waiting for a morsel of food which we could not afford to give him.

I wondered how so many different birds seemed to flourish in this waste of water.

It was that day, June 25, that I began to realise that the success or failure of our row would depend on our mental state and not our physical one.

It was the little things that started to become important. For instance, I had spent eight years in the Army and had shaved every day. It did not matter whether I had been in the field or back in my married quarters with my wife at Aldershot.

But now I was growing a beard, not because I wanted to but because it was impossible to shave every day. It was impossible, partly because of the time it took, but mainly because we could not spare the fresh water to boil up to get a shave.

A beard, when you are not used to one, starts to itch all the time. I found this new beard of mine caught on my clothes, too. I got this tugging effect every time I moved my head. It caught up in my woollen sweater or cotton shirt.

And then the green dye from the tarpaulin kept going all over my hands and face. I would rub at this dye, which seemed to settle most between my fingers. I would get rid of it, but then I found that I had rubbed the flesh between my fingers sore.

These little things I found were the irritating ones, and I knew that I must keep strict control over my feelings of annoyance if I was to keep a stable approach to our row.

I suppose, too, that it was about this time that I started thinking a lot about things that had happened in the past. The simple things like the hills and the land and walking in a wood or fishing—these came to me because they were fresh, pleasant memories which would always stay in my mind.

I wrote in my log: 'Hawick is a very beautiful place —with the hills and rivers. Just to walk along beside the Teviot again. I think a great deal of my mother and how much she really meant to me. My wife, and how I intend to spend the rest of my life with her.'

I was thinking these things that day before John and I were forced to go under the tarpaulin in a three-quarter gale which came up from the south-east. We could not row against that, and although we had got the sea anchor out, we were blowing steadily back towards America.

A German ship, the *Rigoletto*, came over next afternoon when I had used the heliograph to call her. With typical German efficiency her Captain gave us our position and hurried her on her way again.

We had found that we had done only three hundred miles in three weeks, and if we kept on like this John and I reckoned we would finish on January 18, 1967.

Mrs. Moore, the wife of one of the friends we made in America, said before we left, 'Above all you will need patience.'

How right she was. The time seemed to stand still when the wind was against us. We had now lost thirty-six hours of rowing time because of the strong easterly winds and the heavy seas through which it had been impossible to row.

On that Sunday, June 26, we saw eight ships pass close by and one of them stopped. She was the *Robertson II* from St. John, New Brunswick, a Canadian crew who were out for swordfish.

The Captain called down to us, 'Where are you bound for?'

'Falmouth, England,' we shouted back across the calm seas.

'What—in that?'

'Of course—why not?'

'You must be raving mad. I always knew Englishmen were mad. But the best of luck to you, Mac,' he called.

He gave us some very bad news, did that Canadian. The Gulf Stream was still sixty miles away. It was heartbreaking not to have found it after twenty-two days at sea.

On the next day I had a look at John's boil, despite his protestations that I was to leave the thing alone. I found that the dressing had drawn out the boil, root and all. He was very relieved when I told him this, as he had been very worried since we had started about the poison left in his body after his spell in Chelsea Naval Hospital in Boston.

'I don't think you will go rotten yet,' I told him.

On June 28 I saw lightning in the distance at a quarter past eleven in the evening, and I hoped it would not come our way. But it did.

It started at five minutes to one with great flashes followed by claps of thunder some ten seconds later. As the minutes went by so it got closer, and what worried me was the fact that we were the only thing near for the lightning to strike.

It was black, pitch black except for the tiny light from the compass, then a flash turned the whole ocean into daylight for a fifth of a second. Then came the clap and the roar of thunder. All I could do was to row and pray.

I became very frightened indeed, and when I found that John, who was under cover, was awake, I called to him and said, 'Are we going to be all right—this lightning must strike us at some time.'

'Get on with it, Chay, it's only a thunderstorm,' he called out.

It was all right for him, for apart from the lightning and the thunder the rain poured out of the heavens and I was drenched. This went on for fifty minutes, which seemed like five hundred, but by a quarter to two the storm had passed us by.

I was very glad to change places with John, then the fear gave way to sleep.

'Mental plonk'

John Ridgway: July 1–8

WHEN we started out, indeed from the very moment when Chay and I first discussed our voyage one Saturday in my office at the Parachute Regiment Depot both of us realised that many dangers would face us on our long voyage across the North Atlantic.

Gales, heavy seas, sickness—any one of them could turn our adventure into a disaster in which we could lose our lives. Naturally, we prepared for these possibilities to the utmost of our ability. We chose a sound boat. We could navigate and we carried with us a full supply of equipment and provisions, so that we could face almost any emergency with confidence.

We had discussed the venture in military fashion, setting down our objective: i.e. to cross the ocean in the least possible time. We had detailed the methods we would employ to carry out the mission with the least discomfort and greatest safety.

At sea both of us therefore dedicated ourselves to the task in hand and would allow for no time-wasting deviation which would thwart or even delay our purpose. Of course, there was nothing we could do about adverse winds and seas, but our minds were made up that there would be no lack of effort on our part to bring about the end of our purpose in as speedy a manner as possible.

For that reason we carried no books on board, the possibility of our ever having time for reading never entering our heads. As it turned out, there were times when we were unable to row and we had to take shelter against the worsening elements, but even this time was employed in assessing our position and making plans to deal with the unexpected.

We were out there to row—and row we did. During the day we rowed together. At night, after a meal, we took two-hour turns—'stags' we called them—throughout the night.

Even the unexpected occurrence which at first was treated as a minor calamity—such as getting a soaking when waves lapped over the side and somehow always found a way through our suits—became in the end part of the monotony of our routine. This monotony, and the far-reaching effect it would have on us, mentally and physically, was a factor for which we were not able to prepare. Not until we had been at sea for some weeks did I suddenly realise that, physically, we were becoming automatons and, mentally, cabbages.

Of all the perils which faced us on the crossing, this strange malady which afflicted us, this enemy we could not see, was the most dangerous. We called it 'mental plonk'.

Our efficiency so far as the boat was concerned was, I think, unimpaired. We dealt with things as they happened, and we moved fast when we had to. But we went about our work automatically, so familiar had we become with the pattern of the wet, cold and hungry life we had made for ourselves.

Our thinking was devoted to the running of the boat. We wasted no time on what might have been, and there was never any whining from either of us, even in the moments of deepest depression, when we wished we had never started. Hour after hour, day after day, we pulled at those oars, the only sound around us being the creaking from the rowlocks and the gurgle and hissing of the sea sweeping beneath us.

This brought about a kind of hypnosis. For hours we would both sit there, pulling and straining, perhaps not leaving our seat for a second and not exchanging a word. Then, when one of us did say something, it was so unexpected that the other took some time to react to the strange new noise he was hearing.

There would be a pause. A long pause. And the reaction from the other would be something like this, with a half-second hesitation between every word.

'I—didn't—quite—hear—what—you—said. Say—it—again.'

There would be another pause, perhaps of several seconds, before the words were repeated—and so the rather idiotic conversation would go on. At least, it seems daft now. At the time it was quite normal, and I do not think either of us fully realised how completely this weird condition of mind had overtaken us.

We knew that our mental processes had taken a strange turn, that we were thinking and speaking and moving with an unusual deliberation. We both tried to make allowances for this in our relationship, although sometimes it could lead to differences between us, especially when one had slept extra well and felt brighter and more refreshed than the other.

One morning, for example, after preparing our breakfast of the inevitable rice pudding and cocoa, Chay saw that our cooking stove was in our way and suggested to me it should be moved—after all, I was nearest to it. Looking back, it must have looked and sounded like a slow-running movie film, for he said slowly and with a kind of stutter between every syllable, 'I think we should move that stove, John.'

I heard. But the words had no meaning. It did not even occur to me to ask him to repeat what he had said —and it apparently did not occur to Chay to repeat the suggestion. The words must have seeped gradually through to my brain, for several minutes later I replied, in the same monotone and at the same half speed, 'I think you're right.'

Heads turned slightly towards each other, while we still continued to row, two blank faces turned face to face. Gravely the problem was chewed over in silence, until one of us managed to summon up the effort to extend an arm and put the offending appliance out of the way.

'Plonk' of this kind meant that nothing worried us. But I knew it could lead to the more dangerous stage when nothing mattered, and this, we were sensible enough to realise, could bring the whole project to a disastrous end. In such a state of mind it was quite easy to ignore personal cleanliness, keeping the boat ship-shape, and paying due regard to our day-to-day position and progress by the accurate use of our sextant and charts.

We found that things which at first irritated us, even nauseated us, no longer bothered us. We found that our water, for example, contained lumps of a kind of soggy cotton-wool, a marine growth of some sort, I suppose, and at first it was almost impossible to drink. In our state of 'plonk' we just did not care. I would not even bother to try to fish it out of my cocoa. I would simply point to it, tip in another spoonful of sugar to kill the taste, stir it and drink it with relish.

There is little doubt that our reduced rations had a great deal to do with the state of 'plonk' into which both of us had slipped by the time we had been at sea a month.

Many of our provisions had been soaked and rendered useless during Hurricane Alma, and from then on we were committed to short rations giving us little more than two thousand calories a day—about half what was reckoned to be sufficient for our well-being. Being cheerful about this was an effort, but in some ways our state of mind produced a kind of zany, sick humour that would keep us amused for hours. Chay was the official cook, although we took turns for most of the trip, and he could not resist any opportunity of providing a cabaret when serving our rations.

July 1 was a very fine day indeed. The sea was calm and a fierce sun shone out of an azure sky. At about 11 a.m. I suggested to Chay that it was time for a bite to eat. He stood up unsteadily in the rolling boat, placed an old piece of filthy rag over his arm, bowed with a grave dignity that befitted the head waiter of a five-star hotel and said, 'Where would you like it served, sir—in the lounge? Or may I suggest you take it on the terrace on such a fine day as this?'

I laughed so much I almost let go of the oars—and laughed again a few moments later when Chay produced our 'snack'. 'Elevenses is served, sir,' he said. 'The caviar is tophole, but I'm afraid the toast is a little burnt.'

In his hand he held my share of the ration he had split for 'elevenses'—a one-inch square of cheese. I opened my mouth and quickly popped it in, a small tit-bit that would not have fed a mouse, but to me it was as delectable as Chay's imaginary caviar. I rolled it round my mouth, extracting from the smooth outer surface every lick of flavour, before gently nibbling into it and sucking away every molecule to a glutinous liquidity which seemed to seep into every hungry pore in my body.

The whole trip had become an ordeal, but both of us knew that there was no turning back. Of course, we had an emergency transmitter, and with it we could have sent an S.O.S. which would have brought shipping and aeroplanes quickly to our assistance. This we were determined not to do. We had complete confidence in the boat and in each other, and we settled down for a six months' voyage if necessary. This was our game, really, a contest of endurance. We knew we could win it.

And so we rowed on one man at the oars all night long. Chay was rowing on the night of July 4 when the wind began to build steadily. I was sleeping, curled up miserably on the floorboards of 'Rosie', when, suddenly, I was shocked awake.

'It's a white-out,' Chay shouted at me, and that was exactly what the sea looked like, the same kind of absolute white in all directions that dazzles skiers. A huge wave had just broken over us. I was still fighting to get my bearings when a second monstrous wave hit us. 'Rosie' was lifted by the sea and dashed along through the white spray as though we were shooting a rapids. The fluorescence in the water sparkled like snow in the sun.

I took over the oars and Chay went under cover. It was the first time either of us felt the 'ostrich effect'. When our heads were under the canopy we somehow felt safe, no matter what kind of hell was breaking loose two feet away.

For the next two hours I sat there in absolute exultation. It was one of the great moments of my life. Again, my safety and my life had been taken out of my hands. There was nothing I could do except sit back and watch what was happening. It was like skiing in the dark. 'Rosie' would soar up on a great wave, and then we would slide down the slope and I could see the stern rise up against the sky until the silhouette of the rudder would be clawing for the stars.

The sound of movement of the storm and the boat became something like an orchestra. It was wonderful. I am sure I was sitting there with a great grin on my face. I thought, if I am going to die, this is the way to do it—going right through the front door, instead of being run over by a motor car.

But our objective was to row the Atlantic, and our minds were made up to finish the course—unless by some sheer passage of bad luck we still found ourselves rowing into the middle of the autumnal gales, in which case our chances of survival would be very small indeed.

As we rowed we tried to create—whenever our mental 'plonk' allowed—a number of diversions to take our minds off the never-ending tedium. Often we would see a ship passing in the distance and we would look at our watches and say, 'Dinner's nearly ready—wonder what they're eating?' Then we would have a great game of guessing. We would start with the soup and the hors-d'œuvre and continue to the coffee and brandy stage. Sometimes we would even pretend that we could actually see the food being served and deliberately have an argument about the contents of the various dishes.

When we saw a tanker coming toward us—it turned out to be the Liberian ship the *Liquilady*—Chay piped up, 'Look, John, bacon and eggs for breakfast—and I can see the cook's got a leg of pork there for lunch.'

I looked closely at the ship, as if with X-ray eyes. 'That's not pork, you fool,' I said. 'That's a leg of lamb.'

The tanker, which was bound for Montreal, hove to and gave us our position, then continued on her way. The meeting gave our spirits a tremendous spurt. It made us feel that much nearer to home.

I was pleased about this, because for a few days Chay had been in some pain with a swollen thumb which was clearly poisoned. Every jerk of the oars sent pain through his hand and arm, and several times I heard him clench his teeth and stifle a cry. He had been taking one of the pain-killing drugs we carried with us, but the treatment did not seem to be doing much good. Our great fear was that the pain would cause him to slacken his grip on the oar in a rising sea and catch a crab. If that had happened, the oar could have whipped back into his chest and inflicted a serious injury which would have made our position much worse with only one of us able to row. Thankfully, after a few days of taking tablets of tetracycline, the thumb healed and he was able to row normally.

By this time we were well into the Gulf Stream and being helped along at a great rate of knots. The wind was in our favour and we scudded along as if we were on a giant switchback, some of the waves rising to a height of thirty or forty feet. It was almost like surfing, and as we sped up one wave and at breakneck speed down the next, with the white-flecked spume flying in our faces, we both yelled out with excitement and delight. If one could forget that we were in fact way out in the Atlantic and battling for our lives, it might almost have seemed that we were on holiday.

As the boat raced through the water, rising and falling in long undulations, we sang, laughed and felt that we wanted it to go on for ever. I remember Chay singing 'The Road to the Isles' and I replied with 'The Campbells are Coming', then both of us sang 'Colonel Bogey' in unison—the words of which are, I think, peculiar to Army messes.

Thrilling though this kind of progress was during the day, after dark it became a nightmare. Those same waves which in daylight were friendly vehicles of fun, became under the blackening sky giant hands ready to snatch you, boat and all, into a watery grave. The very sound of these great monsters moving with the speed of racehorses and making a noise that words cannot really describe was terrifying and made sleep impossible. When it was my time to creep beneath the canopy, while Chay took his two-hour turn at the oars, I would lay there with eyes closed saying over again and again a prayer for our safety.

Several times a night huge waves would crash down on our little boat, swamping whoever was rowing and falling like a rotten tree on the canopy and shooting water as from a hydrant on to whoever lay under it. It was impossible to do anything about drying the boat out. When it was time to change 'stags' whoever had been rowing would crawl into a small swimming pool. In such miserable conditions we could only hope for a warm breeze and perhaps some sun the following day to dry us out. Sometimes we were lucky enough for this to happen.

In such heavy seas there was always the danger that some hidden harm might befall our boat—perhaps a bent rudder for example—and I decided it was imperative that the underneath of the boat should be inspected as soon as possible.

After one particularly bad night, when the boat was smashed from every direction by waves that seemed to grow hourly in size and power, flat calm came with the dawn and a coppery sun shone through the clouds. I was not grateful for it—the heat was oppressive. My log records: 'I prefer the crash and bang of the sea to this accursed calm.'

I told Chay, 'I'm going in for a swim'—concealing from him the real purpose of the exercise.

Chay said, 'If you're going in, so am I.' He added, 'I know you're not going in for the benefit of your health. I think I should go in to do whatever you want done. After all, I am the better swimmer.'

'But what about those enormous sharks that came around the boat a few days ago? Supposing one of those comes along.'

'Well, I'll get out fast. You can be my lookout.'

I told him that I thought I should go, since I would probably have a better idea of what to look for than he. He persisted in saying he should go first, so in the end I had to say jokingly, 'Look, I'm the skipper of this boat. I insist on going.'

Chay agreed—so long as I promised to let him go in afterwards.

I stripped and dived over the side into the beautiful warm water of the Gulf Stream. It was like a tepid bath, and I lay on my back and luxuriated in it for some minutes while Chay looked on enviously.

'Hurry up,' he said. 'If you don't, I'll come in with you'—and in no time at all he had stripped all his clothes off and poised himself on the gunwales to dive in.

Naturally, he would not have been so foolish as to leave the boat unmanned. It was just one of the ways that he brought his humour into play, as he so often did, to lighten the tension and give us a laugh.

I dived beneath the boat and experienced the most eerie sensation. There I was, hundreds of miles out in the middle of the Atlantic, in water about two miles deep, swimming about as if I was in the sea at Bournemouth, and all the time we knew that sharks and other monsters could not be far away, for we had seen them most days and nights.

I swam through the dark, deep blue water, into which the sunlight penetrated to several feet, and was able to inspect the hull. There was nothing wrong and, surprisingly, no barnacles. I examined the rudder and found that it was untouched by the recent bad weather. I wanted to get back on the boat as quickly as possible, fearing all the time a shark would suddenly cut through the water. I decided, as I examined the boat, that after Chay's dip neither of us would go in the water again.

I got to the surface again with a gasp and spent another couple of minutes basking in the warm sun, while Chay took my photograph. Then he shouted, 'Come on, hurry up. My turn to have a go.' I told him to wait another minute or two, but he was so impatient that he again threatened to dive in at once.

'Number Thirty-four,' I shouted at him. 'I order you to stay where you are.'

'Okay, Number One,' said Chay, and finally, when I was back in the boat, he got his swim.

That was what we called the 'Numbers Game'. It began on our second day at sea. Until that time Chay and I had tended to stick to our military relationship. I would at times call him Chay, but more often I addressed him as 'Blyth', especially in public.

Clearly, it would have been absurd to have continued this at sea. After all, we were equal partners in the rowing of *English Rose III*. On the other hand, our military training inhibited the ready use of Christian names, although later on in the trip we became quite used to calling each other 'John' and 'Chay'.

On the second day of the trip, Chay settled any embarrassment by calling me 'Number One'. I in turn called him jocularly 'Number Fifty'.

'Why so high a number?' asked Chay.

'Because you're a beginner at this lark,' I told him. 'When you've got more experience I'll bring you down to Number Forty—maybe even lower than that.'

It was good for a joke on many occasions to while away the odd anxious or monotonous moment. He stuck on 'Number Thirteen' for a long time, but by the end of the voyage I would say he was a 'Number One' too.

In between these spells of humour there were many anxious moments. The fear of being swept overboard was one of our main worries, and this would undoubtedly have happened if I had not insisted on the use of our life-lines at all times when we were rowing. Towards the end of the trip this rule was relaxed as we became more used to moving about the boat, but at night when only one man was rowing the line was used without fail.

Daily we listened to the radio, mainly to check our watches with time signals, or to listen to some special programme that both of us wanted to hear. We often tuned in to a concert from the Royal Festival Hall, or from America. If we were lucky we heard a concert. Often, however, try as we might to better the reception, the programme was spoiled by atmospherics and we just switched off.

When we were nearer to America reception from there was naturally better—except that most of the programmes were news bulletins and, frankly, we both got fed up with listening to the same old topics. After our third day of listening to nothing but news bulletins, Chay pulled his oars inboard and said—and I afterwards agreed with him, 'Do we have to listen to that stuff all the time about Viet Nam and the American colour problem? We've got enough problems of our own at the moment. We can catch up with the troubles of the world when we reach dry land.'

I switched off the radio and we did not listen to it much afterwards, apart, as I have said, to check the time. Frankly, I think we both received enough entertainment from each other's company—apart from the necessity of keeping an eye on our progress and ensuring that we kept to our main task—rowing.

We also quickly found that, when the opportunity presented itself, our own conversation was the best tonic of all and helped to overcome the many disappointments that must inevitably arise on a journey of that sort.

Food was a subject which was never far from our minds, from early in the morning, when we ate our rice pudding, to the unvarying evening meal of dehydrated curry, I think most of the conversation for the ninety-one days we were at sea turned to the subject of food. We began talking about it in earnest after Hurricane

Alma had passed and our daily food ration was cut by half. I said to Chay, as he pulled on his oilskins to take the first 'stag' of the night, 'I'll tell you what, Chay. As soon as we get back I'll stand you and Maureen the finest meal of your life. The four of us will go out and we'll make a real night of it.'

'That's a great idea,' he replied. 'Let's talk about what we are going to eat.'

'Avocado pear with lobster for a start,' I said.

'Not keen on the lobster with avocado,' said Chay. 'Prefer avocado on its own, followed by lobster mayonnaise.'

I certainly did not agree with that. I made it quite clear that my preference after the pear was a sole meunière. The conversation would continue on those lines for days and weeks, both of us giving the subject of food our every attention whenever it was mentioned.

It took, I think, about five weeks of constant day-to-day discussion to decide exactly what our ideal meal would be when we returned to Britain.

It was a dream that rarely left our minds. The atmosphere and warmth and plushness of a good restaurant, with waiters hovering in attendance and the subdued music—that was a picture in our minds we could not erase. It became the carrot in front of the donkey's nose that kept us going.

How seriously we took the discussion on food can be gauged from the fact that, about a day after we had finally agreed on the meal we should have (avocado, smoked salmon, Aylesbury duckling with orange sauce) Chay suddenly said to me as I was making a midday 'mash' of dried potato and fish, 'We're idiots, aren't we?'

'Why?' I said, interrupting my cooking for a second.

'Because we haven't decided where we are going to eat. We've forgotten about that. Well, haven't we?'

'Okay, okay,' I said. 'We'll get down to that when

we've had this, or this (indicating the mess with my thumb) might get spoiled by the vision of that.'

We took the discussion quite seriously. I suggested a little restaurant I know near Baker Street. I described it in some detail to Chay and read out, as well as I could remember (for Chay is something of a student of wines) the wine list.

'If they haven't got a decent Burgundy, we're not going there,' he said. I suggested another place in Jermyn Street. It seemed to meet with his approval, especially when I told him a small band was usually in attendance.

'That's fine,' he said. 'Maureen and I can have a dance. Marvellous. Can't wait to get there.'

'That's on,' I said. 'That's where we'll go.' At that moment a huge wave hit us, nearly swamping the boat, and for the next hour or so we took turns at the pump and the subject was almost forgotten. But Chay had remembered an Important Point.

'Didn't you say we'd use a car to get up from Alder-shot?' he asked with a quizzical look.

'Yes,' I said.

'Well, does this place in Jermyn Street have a car park?'

'No.'

'Well, what's the point of choosing a place where we can't park the car?'

I collapsed with laughter—and nearly lost an oar in the process. Chay, too, saw the funny side of it, rested for a moment on his oars and said: 'John, we must be going mad.'

There were many subjects we discussed on the trip: philosophy, religion, education and travel, to mention just a few. I personally found great value in these con- versations, for Chay is a highly intelligent and per- ceptive person with an attitude to life which is sane and chockful of common sense. We exchanged confidences on many things and found that in some ways we had similar problems and our talks enabled us to get our thoughts straight.

Next to food the one subject we spoke about most was marriage and what it meant to us as individuals. I would look at my watch during the day as I rowed, or when I was doing a lonely night 'stag', or even when I crouched beneath the canopy trying to get warm in our single blanket, and wonder, 'What can Marie-Christine be doing now?'

If it was during the morning I would imagine her taking a bus to the shops, or walking on a fine summer's evening with her mother's two dogs, Tot, a border terrier, and Gustav, the dachshund. Chay would do the same, looking at his watch and telling me what he thought Maureen, his wife, would be doing at that particular time.

When we were most depressed being married and thoughts of our wives helped us tremendously. Often we would write to our wives, although we knew there was never a chance that those letters would be delivered until we actually returned. We wrote two letters especially. These were kept in a watertight container and sealed and placed along with our provisions. If we did get shipwrecked, we hoped that the container with those letters would be found floating somewhere sometime and would find its way to our womenfolk.

One day, after a particularly bad night, when both of us had been occupied at the pumps, taking it in turns to prevent 'Rosie' from becoming completely waterlogged, Chay turned to me, his voice hardly reaching me in the howling wind, and said, 'You know, John, there is one thing I want out of life once we've reached dry land, and that is to stay with Maureen, and never leave her again.'

Our little boat heaved over almost to the gunwales as heavy seas caught us, and I clung desperately, with freezing fingers, to the underneath of the aft thwart to steady myself during the pumping. Somehow I shouted back against the wind: 'Just let me get back to Marie-Christine. I'll never do a stupid thing like this again.'

The wind and the rain eased soon afterwards, so we were able to cease pumping and bailing out and get some rice pudding ready for breakfast. It had been an awful night, so we decided we would be entitled to one or two of our 'goodies'—a boiled sweet and a square of chocolate—a treat we awarded ourselves when our spirits needed a boost.

As we ate our 'goodies' I felt an overwhelming warmth towards my companion, Chay, with whom I had been through so much. Without his help, intelligence and sense of fun, I felt that the storms we had encountered would have fared us much worse.

I held out my hand to him. 'Thanks for everything, Chay,' I said. 'We're going to make this or bust. And I won't forget that night out.'

That pledge, out there in mid-Atlantic, was a spoken vow of determination that needed to be said. It gave us both words to remember in the dark days that still lay ahead.

Chay's hand clasped mine. 'Of course we're going to make it,' he replied. 'We're just going to keep going until we do. Like those boils we keep getting. We'll keep them till they get better. Everything will be okay in the end.'

Our progress at that stage—about July 7—was not quite as good as we would have wished. We were aiming at a degree a day—or about—and so far we had not covered that, but often the winds were not in our favour and we had to fight constantly against a drift to the north.

I began to feel that we were carrying too much weight and that we would get along much better if we jettisoned some of our water supplies. The idea of doing this appalled Chay. When I told him that I intended to let go about twenty-five gallons, he thought that I was quite mad and that without it we would die of thirst.

Before sailing we had been advised that we would need something like a gallon a day each for all purposes, but after being at sea for thirty-two days we discovered we had used only twenty-five gallons. I therefore decided to lighten our load and hope for greater progress by releasing some.

This I did, to Chay's complete astonishment, but we soon found that there was ample fresh water for our needs and we would still be able to use some for our daily wash, as well as our once a week 'wash-down' and shave.

The weekly wash-down was a ritual to which both of us looked forward as a child does to Christmas. We prepared for it days in advance, and when the great moment arrived the excitement on board was terrific.

First of all there would be a discussion to decide who would take first turn, then one of our polythene bags of water would be tipped into our green plastic bucket, which we used for a variety of purposes on the trip. Then washing would commence. Splashing and yells as the body was cleansed and the encrusted salt on the skin was rinsed off. This was followed by a shave, a normal-life chore which to us was a great luxury.

On one occasion, with the bucket full of water and a bar of soap at hand ready for the weekly ablutions, it began to blow half a gale and the wind whipped up the sea into a boiling mass all round the boat. We decided to delay the wash-down until conditions were calmer—but

95

after a few minutes the sight of that bucket of water and the soap was too much for me, I'm afraid. I could not resist it. I stripped off and leant over the side of the tossing, rolling boat and rinsed off as per schedule. I had tied my lifeline—twenty-five feet of nylon rope—round my middle and, without another care in the world, began to wash.

I thought Chay was unusually quiet. Usually he was full of chatter and good humour at this time of the week, waiting excitedly and impatiently for his turn to wash.

Suddenly he said, 'John—can you stand up a minute —I want to have a look at the line round your waist.'

Thinking that it had come adrift, I stood up for him to inspect it. 'Turn round,' he said. I did so, looking down to see what was wrong.

Suddenly he laughed and pointed. In the distance was a ship. 'I hope there was somebody on deck with binoculars to get a good view of you,' he said. 'They might stop.'

Perhaps the sight of me—if anybody on that boat had been watching—frightened them off. Anyway, the ship did not stop, as we had hoped. I stopped my washing and waved. Chay tied an anorak to the wireless mast and held an oar in the air, waving and shouting—but the ship steamed on without seeing us.

We were not surprised. It had happened many times before. Ships seemed to pass within a few hundred yards of us and, despite our frantic efforts to attract attention, we were not seen. It made us feel even more lonely to know that on the wide expanse of the ocean we were nothing more than a splinter of wood.

It was becoming more and more imperative to stop a ship and take on fresh provisions. We worked out that even with the most economical use of all the food on board—including our emergency storm rations—we still had enough for only forty-eight days. And I began to doubt whether we would last that long on a weakening diet. A typical day's ration at this stage of the journey (the first week in July, after being at sea just over a month) was:

Midday: a plate of rice pudding each and half-pint of cocoa. Evening: curry and two ounces of rice, with half-pint beef cube drink. Our 'goodies'—boiled sweets such as Spangles, chocolate bars and fudge—were also strictly rationed and were generally consumed during the night 'stags'.

I had lost a few pounds in weight. I tried to tell myself that I had 'fined down' and rid myself of surplus flesh and was healthier for it. But I knew this was not the case. The diet we were on was barely sufficient for a healthy living standard on shore; it was certainly having an effect on our health at sea with the tremendous amount of physical and nervous energy we were expending each day.

There could be no let-up from rowing to try to recover our strength. I realised that once we began to take things easy our state of 'mental plonk' would become even more acute and might even lead to our lying in the bottom of the boat and praying to die.

Our mental and physical well-being could be prevented from slipping further only by our carrying on and hoping that a ship would stop before it was too late. I do not think either of us really despaired, but I had begun to dread the nights when I was alone with only my thoughts in that awful damp so-called bed under the canopy. Would we ever escape from this hell? Yes, of course we would, I kept telling myself. But when? I could find no answer to that.

We tried each day to find a highlight which would give us a little amusement, or some event to which we could look forward—the opening of a new bar of chocolate, for instance, and wondering whether its flavour would be slightly different from the last. Although neither of us are drinkers, we had on board one bottle of whisky and a bottle of wine. We carried these mainly for their medicinal value, but their true worth, psychologically, was inestimable.

They were there to drink when we had something to celebrate. We intended to drink the wine when we talked to our first ship—but we let the *Liquilady* go without bothering to crack the bottle. We thought we might be tempting providence if we celebrated too early on the voyage, so we thought we would open a bottle after the first five hundred miles. When we reached that point our progress seemed so insignificant that we just did not bother. Instead, we made up our minds to open a bottle on my twenty-eighth birthday, July 8.

It was still a terrific battle to hold our position. We were making steady progress in the right direction—east —but gale-force winds from the south-west were knocking us to the north. My birthday, therefore, was not a day of relaxation.

'Happy birthday,' said Chay as he prepared an early morning snack of rice pudding. 'We're going to have our work cut out.' He was right. The skies were overcast and a steady drizzle fell. The early morning winds caused us to ship quite a bit of water and our breakfast was forgotten while we bailed out.

Physical activity in every form was becoming more difficult. Both of us had sore bottoms and thighs from the continual chafing in salt-sodden clothing which never seemed to be dry, and our hands were often red-raw where callouses had been rubbed off to expose the tender under-skin.

It was far from being a happy birthday. I felt run-down and knew that the 'plonk' was affecting both of us. We were getting on each other's nerves, and several times came near to harsh words. The weather was worsening and there was plenty to do, what with the rowing, preparing food and warm drinks and tidying the boat.

We rowed together for most of the day, and my birthday was not mentioned again. Our whisky and bottle of wine lay forgotten—not that either of us had the inclination or the capacity to try even a sip. Supper time came and went. I washed our pressure cooker, which was the only cooking and eating vessel we had, and prepared to tuck down for a couple of hours while Chay took the first 'stag'.

I closed my eyes and wanted nothing more than to drift off into black unconsciousness. Chay said something to me, but the words did not register. It was something about the rudder, but it did not occur to me to ask him to repeat what he said. After a minute or so he said it again. Ah, yes, he wanted the rudder lashed farther to port. I just snuggled down more into my blanket.

I was not being cussed. It was, quite simply, that Chay's words would take a few minutes to register before I moved to comply with his request. Eventually, they did so, and I crawled slowly from the 'bed' and moved the rudder as Chay had asked. I then crawled back under my blanket.

After another minute or two I could hear Chay's voice again. It dawned on me that he was saying I still had not set the rudder correctly and would I do something about it? I heard every word he said, but the malfunctioning of my body was such that I just lay there staring at him. This was 'plonk' at its worst when for several minutes there was simply no co-ordination between brain and body.

Slowly, I replied, 'It can wait until morning.'

It was a foolish thing to say. Of course, I was quite wrong. The setting of the rudder was of paramount importance to the running of the boat, and I can offer no excuse other than that I was stricken with this amazing malaise that neither of us could have foreseen before we started out.

Gales and storms we could reckon with—but 'mental plonk' was a hidden danger that neither of us ever expected. After another minute or so of rowing, Chay leaped from his seat blurting a string of oaths. 'Blast you then,' he shouted. 'If you can't fix the rudder properly, I'll do the damn thing myself.'

Those were the first strong words that had passed between us. For several minutes I continued to lay there while I pondered on this rift that had suddenly come between us. The whole thing was my fault, and I was desperately sorry.

Another few seconds' silence. Then both of us spoke together.

'I'm sorry, John,' said Chay.

'I'm sorry, Chay,' said I.

Our first and only row was over. I turned over and slept, happier than I had been at any time that day.

Whales and dolphins

Chay Blyth: July 9–17

THAT was our first quarrel, if you can call it that, and it was the only one we ever had. Pretty good, really, when you consider that John and I were never more than a few feet from each other for three months, living under conditions which were not exactly soothing to the temper. Dozens of times he exasperated me by doing some small, insignificant thing, and I felt like roaring at him. There must have been just as many times when he felt like cursing me.

But we both realised the danger of losing our tempers. We talked about it before we left Cape Cod.

'Patience, patience, patience,' I would repeat to myself, and it was soon easy to swallow my anger.

I woke John up twice late on Saturday night. It was foggy and I could hear a ship coming ever closer. I suggested we put up the radar reflector, but John said not to bother. It needed two of us to do this. One would have to stand on the gunwales to do the fixing, and the other hang on to him to stop him falling in. We did this when we had to tighten rudder ropes, or get to the sea anchor over the bow.

Anyway, the ship passed well over to the North. I went on rowing for forty-five minutes, then I heard a sound like a long, drawn-out phewwwww. A kind of whooshing of air being let out. In no time at all, there were five whales circling the boat. Round and round they went, great smooth beasts, hardly making any splash at all.

I suppose they were quite small, really—about the size of an average car. But they certainly made me flap. So I shook John again.

'Don't worry,' he said. 'They'll be all right.'

I knew why he wasn't worried. He was underneath the canopy and had the 'ostrich feeling', as we called it. It's psychological, secure. You think, 'I'm all right. I'm under cover. Nothing can hurt me.'

But I was not so confident. I kept wondering what would happen if one of the whales decided to surface right underneath 'Rosie'. Perhaps he would give us a lift to Land's End. It was not a very funny joke, but it made me feel a little better.

The great hulks swam to about seven yards from the boat. Then they went away. Soon two of them returned, circling the boat, gradually coming closer. I stopped rowing. I would have actually hit one of them with the boat if I hadn't. Obviously they were simply curious. I wondered whether they thought 'Rosie' was another sort of whale.

During the day we rigged up an aerial to help us get the Washington time signal better. This was essential for estimating our longitude. Navigation had become a little tricky, as we never seemed to have visibility for a sight at noon. So latitude had to be estimated.

We were both pretty tired, but were sleeping well now. John talked about his body. He thinks of it as a car body with a big engine which takes a little warming-up.

'I think it's a good machine,' he told me. 'But it needs quite a bit of tuning for a stint like this.'

He fished an excellent polythene jar out of the sea, and we decided to use it to keep our log pages and film in.

The water temperature was changing constantly, and John said this indicated the twisting-turning vagaries of the Gulf Stream. He believed it sometimes turns back on itself.

My feet were in better shape than his. We both had size ten Wellington boots, but I take size eight and he takes size ten. I could get two pairs of socks on with mine. His were cushioned only by one pair.

In the night the compass light went out. Corrosion, I supposed. It was very annoying, because there were no stars. We tried to judge the direction we were going, first of all, using the torch. Then we got on course, put the torch down, rowed and attempted to keep 'Rosie' at the same angle to the waves. Frustrating, and unsatisfactory. But without the stars it was the best we could do.

We did not have enough batteries to keep the torch on all the time. So every ten minutes it was stop rowing, grab the torch, check the compass, correct course and start again. It took only a few seconds. But we had to stop rowing, and the boat lost momentum.

Next day it was very hot, but there was a faint breeze which stopped it from being too intense. I was fiddling with the radio when, without warning, an English voice came out through the crackling. John and I grinned at each other. It was marvellous to hear good, plain English talking. The man said it was the B.B.C. Overseas programme. We left it on, savouring every item. From then on we played the radio a lot more.

We took it in turns to row. I washed and shaved and scrubbed my red track suit. We made up our minds to live with the continual wetness from the condensation inside our suits, instead of trying to cure it. I felt a great deal better once I got mine off and let it flap in the air for a while. John had a big clean up too, and we both felt more relaxed.

The clothes steamed in the sun, and I thought it would not be long before Maureen would be hanging out the washing at home. Suddenly I very much wanted to see that washing.

John was worried about his spots. They were all over his bottom and creeping a third of the way up his back. Fortunately, I wasn't bothered with them yet. John put cream on them and we both used alcohol spirit to try to dry the skin. In his log John wrote: 'Every minor chafe or sore is a cause for long-term concern. We could walk off this boat today and after a shower no one would be able to tell what we had been through unless they looked at our hands.' Our hands were getting very hard. Rows of callouses built up, then our hands got wet and they would peel off—little discs of compressed skin. They soon hardened again.

John wrote in his log: 'I wish the west wind would come. We are in excellent heart and will see this through. Missed the Mer Alt sight owing to fog but assessed 43 degrees North as near and worked out 51 degrees 14 minutes longitude in the afternoon. We have done ten degrees west in ten days and are going to do better and better.'

We found the glucose drink gave us lots of energy. If we drank a lot we did not have to eat so much. Rations worried us, but we thought we should be able to last out a further fifty days. Both of us had lost weight, but we were in excellent condition. John wondered if we were already too light, and would become run down during the next forty-five days. I did not think we would.

The fog came back in the morning, and with it, the east wind. Most of our clothes became soggy with dampness.

We pulled together against the wind and it was like rowing into a wall of darkness. By the evening my hands were sore and there was a stabbing pain in my left forearm. In the night I heard a ship's fog-horn. It is a weird, forlorn sound. I imagined the men on board, sitting around their wooden table, scooping up huge spoonfuls of steaming stew, joking, perhaps, about the four men who were trying to row the Atlantic in two small boats.

I saw some fish which I thought were dolphins. Quite small—about six foot long—and roundish. They seemed to have white stripes on their bellies and had small dorsal fins with half-moon tails, rising horizontally.

We ate meat bars, emergency rations, barley sugar blocks and goodies. All washed down with half a pint of glucose and water. Just over 2,000 calories, I suppose. Not enough really. It fell below 1,250 in July.

The oars we got in America, each one carved from a single piece of ash or oak, gave us a little concern. They looked as if they were wearing down. We had lost one oar, and the four we were using now lost their rubbing strips within twenty-four hours. However, we were to learn that they would stand up wonderfully to tremendous usage.

This, Monday, July 11, was our thirty-eighth day at sea.

Fog cleared the next day, and John took careful sightings. He spent quite a time working out that we should finish the trip in another forty-three days. Almost halfway! It quite cheered me up.

At seven o'clock we saw about a hundred dolphins or porpoises, four to five feet long, streaking along, jumping out of the waves. An hour later I was rowing on my own while John cooked the breakfast, when I looked up and saw a shark.

'John,' I said, 'we'ye got a dark fellow with us.'

He really was a massive shark, with a huge dorsal fin. Easily the biggest we saw. John grabbed the camera and managed to take a few photographs before he slowly sank out of sight.

I made a big mistake then. It seems piffling when I think about it now. But for two men in a boat it wasn't. At the time it seemed so serious that I recorded it in my log: 'Eat John's Enerzades by mistake—still no friction.'

It could have caused quite a rumpus. But he was very good about it. He simply said, 'Chay, you realise you've eaten my Enerzades,' and left it at that.

Anyway, when the next day's goodies came out I insisted on giving him a packet of mine. I felt better after that.

Changing over 'stags' was really quite funny. The one who had completed his two hours' rowing would be very cheerful and give a brisk run-down on the situation. The chap who had just woken up would look as though doomsday had come, and two hours later it would be just the reverse.

We cut down drastically on food now, and we tried to lengthen our sleep by one man eating a cold breakfast while the other snoozed on. This did not work. It was light by two o'clock, and we decided a hot meal was essential by eight o'clock. Could our bodies stand up to the reduced diet? We would have to find out.

For breakfast we had scrambled egg, biscuits and glucose. Lunch was sardines and glucose; dinner curried rice, cocoa, and soup. We drank five pints of water.

All day we rowed like fury. We had got to make one degree a day otherwise, when we neared Britain, we should be out of rations. Our palate now was quite acute. We were really tasting the difference between foods.

I had never liked sardines before. Now we both pronounced them great. We would sit facing each other, carefully mashing up the small fish so that all the oil was absorbed. Then we would spoon it into our mouths, slowly and very carefully, so as not to drop a particle.

A dolphin passed us, going like a bullet, as we played the game of seeing who could make his sardines last the longest.

The radio told us that an American had sailed from Florida and landed in Eire. The smallest boat ever, I think the man said—a three and a half metre yacht. And here we were in a twenty-foot dory with no sail. What the devil were we doing?

I started thinking about my motor-cycling days. In my mind I could see myself riding along the open road. I could almost feel the power of the bike between my thighs.

John had been giving me French lessons, so in return I said, 'How would you like to learn to ride a motor cycle?'

'Delighted,' he said. 'But the road looks a bit wet to me.'

'No trouble,' I said. 'Pretend the thwart is your saddle. Each one of the oars is a handlebar. On the right-hand handlebar is your throttle and front brake. On the left is your clutch and air control.'

I twiddled my fingers to show him how things worked. He soon began to get the hang of it, and a couple of lessons later he was doing very well. 'When we land,' he said, 'I'll race you across country for a pound.'

We were really out in mid-Atlantic now, and there were very few ships. It would be good to meet one so that we could get our logs and film back to Aldershot. I wrote: 'To date it's been great. No problems at all. I hope the future is the same.'

John and I were hungry all the time now, but at least we were finding it easier to get up and row our 'stags'.

Came Thursday, and quite early on we managed to get the B.B.C. World Service. Thank God for the B.B.C. It was quite a boost to our morale, as we were both fed up with the Voice of America and U.S. local channels, which are for ever plugging somebody's soap or ghastly breakfast food.

I remember the first things we heard were messages to merchant seamen. If only the announcer would say: 'And now a message for Captain John Ridgway and Sergeant Chay Blyth, somewhere in the Atlantic, from their wives, Marie-Christine and Maureen. . . .' Would they try to send us a message? Would anyone? Doubtful, we thought.

'The shipping strike,' said the man, 'is over.' Cheers! Now perhaps we would meet more ships. 'And now the sports report follows. . . .'

We ate R.A.F. Emergency Rations all day. They made quite a pleasant change really. The oatmeal block was particularly good. We drank more, in case of dehydration, but it did not have any visible effect.

The wind was with us all day. We lashed the rudder, and slowly 'Rosie' gathered speed. The wind gradually got stronger until it was about force seven. There were huge seas. When we were at the bottom of the trough and looked up the waves towered like big black houses.

I had become part of the boat now. So had John. I had learnt to judge, in between the waves, when to move. I watched them closely, chose my moment, moved slowly, deliberately, so that three parts of my body touched the boat at all times—two hands and one foot.

The rules were: Don't rush; don't loosen anything, don't hurt yourself. We kept reminding each other that there was no spares depot, or second-hand shop, around the next wave. We needed what we had now to reach the other side. It was a technique that worked well when we had to change places—or do anything.

We shipped a lot of water, but the excellent pumps spurted it out quickly. In the afternoon John got soaked and had to put on his kit over a wet track suit. The night was not too bad. With the help of the wind your hands do not get so sore.

Sighting was difficult, but John reported our position 'satisfactory'. We must have put in a lot of miles that day.

Gale force eight. We were both wet and cold. The wind kept blowing out the cooker, and we could not really afford the wastage of striking more and more matches. Sometimes we lay in the water as the waves swamped us. The sea filled up our Wellingtons. The chap at the oars concentrated on rowing and steering against the seas. Often the man sleeping had to be shaken and asked to pump out. It was most unpleasant, and worrying because it meant precious minutes of sleep were lost. Everything had to be worked out to the smallest detail now: energy expended, sleep wasted, energy to be conserved.

Our hoods were up all the time, and safety harness was worn continually. In his log John described that day:

'Large waves coming up over the starboard quarter are helpful in so far as they push us along. They also swamp us every half hour or so when the surfing action does not quite synchronise. We now have a peculiar confidence in 'Rosie', who seems to take and shed water, yet keeps headed for home with consummate ease.

'It seems it would take very severe weather, coupled with an unusual wave from an unexpected angle, to turn her over.

'...Our only refuge is the canvas in the stern. We have rigged this about gunwale high and crawl underneath with the rudder lashed at night. Huddled together, we keep each other warm and assure each other that nothing lasts for ever and that we are being pushed in the right direction. I am nearest the pumps and ... can reach over the after thwart and work the handle. I estimate around 7,000 strokes during the hours of darkness. The mental effort to leave the wet warmth of the space blanket, and Blyth, in order to pump when I hear the bucket swilling in the well between the thwarts....'

Wet clothes all next day. The wind, thankfully, was warm. John was rowing when a vast wave flooded us. I leant forward to pump and whack!—a small part of the wave following hit me in the back of the head and flattened me. Only stiffening my arms quickly saved me from injury. I had never before realised the colossal force in a single wave. I knew they sounded like sledge-hammers hitting the side of the boat. Now I knew they felt similarly when they caught you by surprise.

I itched with the damp. It could drive a man crazy. Biting my lip helped a little, but in the end I had to give in and scratch. The blankets were our lifeline. Unfortunately they tore easily when wet. Small holes soon enlarged, and it was vital to keep them in one piece. When I lay down to sleep and found I had to move, I tried to do it ever so gently. But sometimes, when I was restricted and uncomfortable, I forced myself into a new position and zip! the blanket would tear. I think I tore them more than John—something he was continually reminding me of, regardless of who was guilty.

I could not get the cooker going during the day, so we snacked on different rations and drank glucose. In the evening I managed a curry, but the cooking took an age because of the wind. The curry was our worst so far—very lumpy.

My morale was a little low and I was very tired. John and I prayed. We talked about prayer and its power, about having faith. After forty-three days we had learnt that it was not a sign of weakness to pray for our own safety, that it was not wrong to ask for help when things were going badly. Our appreciation of the basic values of life was dramatically sharpened: our faith, our wives, our parents. So much we had taken for granted. Now there was plenty of time to dissect our mistakes.

We chatted about our years of Army training. We recalled the exercises when, cold and wet, we had tried to keep warm. That training was proving invaluable out here, in the big deep.

The sea was so furious that rowing was dangerous. We spent a lot of time simply avoiding getting hurt. Still we skimmed along before the wind, shivering the night away.

I was not bored. Nor was John. We never ran out of conversation. John wrote in his log: 'We both believe that we are nowhere near the end of our tether and that "Rosie" will see us right.'

Watching the trillions of tons of moving water, I sometimes wondered what it must be like to drown. Morbid, perhaps, but natural for a chap who is living just a few inches from water that stretches downwards for a mile or two.

I asked John what he thought. 'Don't fancy it,' he said. We talked about it and failed to comfort ourselves with the thought that everybody said if you had to die, then drowning was recommended. People who have almost drowned, and been revived, are supposed to have said it is a pleasant sensation. Pleasant? The thought of leaving life behind is abhorrent and fearful to me. I have always believed that I will survive. Whatever happens to other people, Blyth will still be around. I still believe it.

Sunday again. July 17. And what a different Sunday from last week. There would be no washing and shaving today. But at last the wind was going down. Thank God for that. It really was awful. I was very cold and very wet, and every inch of my body was one, long, irritating itch. We could not take our suits off, and it was agony to leave them on.

I looked at John, stubbly, grey and grim. His broad nose, flattened by many a boxer's punch, spread across his face. 'Is that,' I asked seriously, 'a Roman nose?'

He looked at me pityingly. 'No, it is not,' he said. He explained that a Roman nose was like so, and so. He talked about the heads of the Caesars and what good examples they provided. It was quite a learned discourse, and he managed to stretch it out for a good five minutes.

I waited until he had finished.

'I see,' I said. 'Well, if that isn't a Roman nose, why is it roaming all over your face?'

Once again, it wasn't a hilarious joke. But it gave us something to chuckle about and made us feel a little better.

I remembered us saying how good it would be if some strong westerlies could come along to propel us before them. Now I was not so sure. I reckoned that for the best speed, force four to five was ideal.

The wind went right down and veered to the Northwest. But it happened too late for us to get dry. Rowing was an ordeal with soaked hands and backsides. John had a form of nappy rash on his bottom, and each stroke was what he called 'interestingly painful'.

A huge shark started shadowing us astern. He looked very sinister in the rough sea, and I did not like the way he was eyeing me. I hoped he was just a harmless basker and was not planning any ramming operations. He appeared capable of it.

Neither of us were sick, and we chewed dozens of hard tack biscuits. We saw two ships, one, a tanker, on the horizon. We stood up in turn, hanging on to the after samson post, to stare at it. One was going East and the other West.

'In four or five days' time they'll be in the United

Kingdom or America,' I said. 'And we've still got at least thirty-nine days to go.'

We thought this was a shipping lane and reckoned our best course was now South-east. The ships were running East-north-east for Europe, so soon we might make contact again.

There were plenty of planes too. I heard them droning overhead and imagined the passengers, comfortable in their plush seats, sipping cocktails, or slicing through huge, juicy steaks, surrounded by green peas and mushrooms. In four hours they would be at the airport, ready to jump into cars and head for their soft, sprung mattresses. I was not complaining though. Hardship, fatigue, stamina, endurance; these were the things I wanted to find out about, and I was doing just that.

The night was clear, and we both saw a dozen shooting stars. They flashed across the sky, like beautiful green flares, disappearing on the horizon. God was putting on a firework display for us. A few days earlier I had seen what I thought to be a green flare. I now realised it was probably a star.

We were using the stars to steer by too. This is particularly tricky when stars on the horizon are used. They often shrink suddenly when seen through the weary eyes of the tired oarsman.

I considered the stars. What force is it that keeps them up there, galaxy after galaxy, suspended in space over myriads of miles? It is awesome. I was still thinking about it when I went to sleep. It was a fairly comfortable night.

Against the easterlies

John Ridgway: July 18–26

IN mid-July with the sun shining the ocean looks like the peaceful waters off Blackpool Pier—it was a gem of a day and one more to add to our memories of the glories of the sea. Of course we took advantage of it; one could not waste a time when the boat was comparatively still and there was an opportunity to move about without being hammered against a thwart or a gunwale by an unexpected twist from 'Rosie'.

We washed and shaved. First the shave, the thing that when finished makes you feel clean and healthy and respectable again—a great morale boost, this. Water was poured carefully from one of the plastic water-bags into our pressure cooker, still a bit greasy from the curry of the night before. Then we flashed up the stove and held the pressure cooker steady to make certain we did not get boiling water over our feet. The luxury of boiling water, poured out into a bucket and steaming away in the fresh sun of a new morning. A dollop of shaving cream, a good lather and away with the safety razor. The boat rolled, the razor slipped, there was a tiny trickle of blood down my chin. But it was soon over. My face was smooth and clean, but a bit sore from the nicks of the razor, and the salt air made the whole face tingle. But how good it felt.

.I grabbed our piece of soap and started cleaning off some of the grime which seemed to collect in the most difficult places. I gave my feet a good going over in the water—the same in which I had shaved—because I was still a little anxious about the swollen foot I had earlier. There were no doctors there, and I wanted to be certain that I did not get another poisoned leg. After the wash I had a good rub-down, used a lot of Army foot powder on my feet—and felt a new man. I could see why our old Colonial officers would dress for dinner in the middle of a jungle—it kept morale up.

Chay had his shave and wash, and I noticed how tanned he was and that his muscles were in good shape. We needed that strength of Chay's—I knew I could never have managed if I was left on my own or if he fell ill.

Our idyll soon passed, because I felt a breath of wind —from the east. Then it set in, a steady blow and from the wrong direction. It was blowing us back and it was much too strong for any progress against it to be made. We wondered what would be the best way of dealing with this, as our progress over the past week had been excellent and we did not want to lose a foot of our advantage. In the end we decided against putting out the sea anchor; we would have one man row all the time just to try to stay in the same position. It meant an enormous amount of sweat and energy without getting one yard nearer to home, and this was really heartbreaking.

I did get a good sight which put us close to Weather Ship *Delta*. As I plotted the new position on our chart, I thought how strong willed the men who man these weather ships must be. All they do for weeks on end is steam around in small circles—the ocean is far too deep to anchor in—put out met. reports, give radio guidance to any passing ship or aircraft.

While I was thinking this the word 'radio' clicked.

'Chay, give me the R/T set and I'll see if we can have a chat with the Weather ship—it's not far away from here,' and our only two-way set was passed on to me.

I pulled out the aerial, switched it on and saw that the light showing that it was operating correctly was shining brightly. All seemed well.

'Hello *Delta, Delta, Delta,* this is the British rowboat *English Rose III* in position 44 degrees 14 minutes North, 41 degrees 23 minutes West. Do you hear me, please, do you hear me, please. Over.'

Chay stopped rowing as he heard me put this call out. He sat tensed forward on the thwarts. Nothing.

I tried again: 'Hello *Delta, Delta, Delta...*'

Three times I tried. Three times I put that call out and pressed the earpiece close to my head, hoping to hear the voice of one of the friendly American Coast-guard men.

'It's no good, Chay—they're just not getting it.' I began to put it away.

'Wait a minute, John, our transmitter might be work-ing okay and the receiver may be US. They may hear us and we just can't hear them. Put another call out with a message—it's a chance and worth taking,' Chay said.

He was right, of course. Again I called *Delta* and sent the message into the blue, 'Please report our position to Lloyds of London and say that we are fit and well. Thank you *Delta*. Out.'

Chay started rowing again, just keeping us in the same position.

'I'm pleased you did that, John. We've been unseen for nearly three weeks, and Maureen and M.C. must be getting anxious. They might get phone calls in the next few hours.... I'd like to see the look on Maureen's face if she got a call to say I was okay.'

I was depressed because I had not been able to raise *Delta*. I knew they kept guard on 2,182 mgs, the emer-

gency R/T wavelength. Or did they? I felt abandoned
—no one really cared where we were, and no one was
listening for us.

I found out later that my message had not been
picked up, so I suppose there may have been something
wrong with the set. That was probably Hurricane Alma
having yet another say in our affairs, I reflected. You
just cannot get away from this fact—the wind and the
seas are your enemies, and they attack you directly in a
frontal drive or they sneak up unawares and stab you in
the back. All is treachery at sea.

I was thinking that when, of course, I was forced to
change my mind—the sea is full of change itself. I saw
strange-coloured seaweed, twisted and curly, a piece of
floating life. I was entranced by the colour and by the
way it seemed to wave at me as it slid by 'Rosie'. Its
fronds fluttered in the ripples on the surface, and I felt
that there was beauty and strangeness at sea as well as
treachery. It all depended how you felt at the time.

The east wind drew my attention again as it freshened slightly and began to blow at about Force 4. I
wondered if one man was enough to maintain our position and thought not—so we both rowed together again
for six hours. I did not know whether we made any progress or whether we were being blown back. But nothing lasted for ever, that was what I kept saying to myself.
Neither could our food—and that was a sobering
thought.

Just to add to my depression about the day I broke the
water thermometer that our friend Earl Hitchcock of
Chatham gave to us. That meant that we would not be
able to tell how cold the water was, and this was a definite disadvantage. The Gulf Stream, flowing with its
warmed-up sea-water from the Gulf of Mexico, is rather
like a river flowing between banks of cold water. It is
of assistance to any craft travelling eastwards, even a

small boat like ours. So if you cannot see the bright blue colour of the water of the Gulf Stream at night a thermometer can tell you if you are in it or not. I was surprised when I was given this information, because I thought that the sea temperature would be roughly the same all over the ocean and only change in the various seasons. But I was assured I was wrong. I was given a good example of an oceanographic vessel plotting ocean currents and flows and temperatures. This particular ship stopped on the western edge of the Stream off the American coast. The temperature of the water at the bow was 72 degrees Fahrenheit. The temperature at the stern, some 300 feet away, was 48 degrees Fahrenheit. So I missed my thermometer. I thought we had had a bad day.

The next day was even worse. The wind got stronger and blew Force 5, and Chay and I slaved away to try not to lose ground. We just had to hang on and wait until some wind came from the West. We sat for hour after hour of monotonous plod, plod, plod, and could have cried at the energy we were expending all to no purpose.

The wind slid round to the South-east, and we began to crab northwards and we still did not do any good. It really was fearfully depressing.

We tried to pass the time planning meals.

'What will you have for your first course, Chay? Soup, or a lobster cocktail, perhaps a plate of smoked salmon or a pile of whitebait. Why not a whole iced melon?'

I felt hungrier with every moment that passed. I could taste that food, I could hear the chefs chattering in the kitchens, hear the plops of wine corks being pulled and the bubbling, golloping sound of wine being poured into a glass.

Then we saw a ship in the dark, rows of lights and the proud shape of a bow thrusting the vessel towards

Europe. It was a world of saneness and comfort. The bunks would be dry and the food hot. You would not get wet on that bridge.

'Chay, let us flash the torch at her, she's bound to see us in the night-time like this. We'll make certain that a message gets to Lloyd's that way.'

'No, Number One, it's too risky at night. It's bad enough being close to a ship in the daytime, but we've only got to make a mistake—or her Captain make a mistake—for us to be crushed. I'd hate the ignominy of being hauled aboard an ocean-going ship after losing our own boat—what would the blokes in the Regiment say?'

We talked it over for a moment or two more, and we compromised. We would call the next ship we saw at night.

The next time I spoke to Chay I made a bad mistake. I called him 'Number Thirty-four', still playing this game of me being Number One and he having his number reduced from fifty downwards.

'What have I done? Just because you're upset at not calling that ship, you've demoted me!'

'What do you mean? I'm all right. I'm not upset.'

'Well, you've got a short memory. It could only have been a couple of hours ago that you promoted me from Number Thirty-four to Number Thirty-two.'

He was right. I had promoted him for his courage. I noticed earlier in the day that once or twice he winced as he rowed. It was hard going, and every time you put an oar into the water a jerk would be transmitted up your arms to your shoulders. Chay went on for hours rowing away steadily. Then he stopped.

'John, where's the lanoline?' he asked me. We scrummaged around and found it.

'What do you want it for?' I asked him when he was unscrewing the top.

'Oh, I've only got a sore finger.'

'Let me look.'

Chay held his hand out to me. I reached for his other hand. I was appalled. All his fingers were swollen, red and covered in tiny splits.

'Clench your fists,' I told him.

'Look, John, just give me the lanoline again and let me get on with it.'

'Clench your fists.'

But he could not. He could close them so far. They were like claws of a bird closing far enough to clutch its perch.

That was it, of course. The tendons and ligaments must have seized up and would only let the fingers clutch an oar. He flexed his fingers and tried to clench his fist again. He still had no luck. There was nothing I could do. It was just an effect of those damned oars and the constant jerking and pulling.

There was one thing I could do, not that it would help much. As Chay rubbed lanoline into his fingers, between the joints, I told him, 'You're Number Thirty-two as from now.'

I was still thinking of those swollen hands when he came up with a very good idea.

'You know we wake our relief at night five minutes before he is due to take over? Well, I've been thinking a lot about this. I don't know how you feel, but I lie there for five minutes dreading the fact that I've got to get out and work hard. It's bad enough when the two of us are rowing in the daytime, at least we have company. But the nights are so miserable.

'Why don't we change this? Let's wake each other two minutes before he's due. Then we won't have time to think. We'll only have time to push back the blanket, struggle to the thwart and take over. We won't have that five minutes of dread.'

'Chay, that's a great idea—we'll do just that.' We did, for the rest of the voyage. I found that by the time I had woken up properly I had taken two or three strokes of the oars and that I had settled in without knowing. It did not make rowing easier, it just cut down the thoughts.

The next time I awoke to south-easterly winds again I began to think that all the experts were wrong and that the prevailing winds were from England and not America. I supposed that the longer it blew from the East, the sooner it would blow from the West. I know that that was a very dubious philosophy, but it helped a bit.

We decided to cheer ourselves up a bit by having a feast for breakfast. I broke open one of our four remaining tins of fruit juice, and we had this with hard tack, margarine and jam. It was very enjoyable. I must say that I never thought I should ever enjoy Army biscuits and margarine. But in 'Rosie' it was a real feast.

Chay and I thought we would settle down that day and write to our wives. I sat on a thwart with my back to that miserable easterly that was still pushing us backwards, and produced some of my yellow, lined exercise book, the stub of pencil that I had been using to make my daily log entries, and started. I tried to start, that is. But how do you start to give reassurance? I knew my wife would see through any chatty 'wish you were here' type of letter. So I concentrated on writing my thoughts about her. I left the rest to her imagination.

When we had finished Chay and I talked about what we would do with the letters. We decided to put them in a watertight container with the first part of our logs and the photographs that we had taken up till then. We addressed the lot to Colin Thomson, my friend with the Parachute Regiment, and marked it 'Cash on Delivery'.

We decided, too, that we would hand this package to the first ship that stopped that was going to England and ask the Captain if he would be kind enough to post it for us.

My wife never did get that letter, neither did Chay's. The first ship that came along was going to North America. We never did meet a ship going to Europe and we felt that there was a good chance of the container going astray if it were posted from North or South America. I suppose this decision at least saved Colin Thomson from stumping up a couple of pounds when the postman called.

Later we settled down to our steady grind at the oars. When I sat and started pulling on the first 'stag' of the night I found that it seemed to last only about ten minutes. I suddenly looked at the watch and saw it was time to shake Chay so he could take over. I could not believe it, and I sat and pondered as soon as I was tucked up into the blanket with Chay taking his 'stag'.

Why, I asked myself, did that watch pass so quickly? I tried to remember any event at all that had occurred during the two hours that I had been rowing. I could remember taking over from Chay and settling into the old routine. I could remember looking at the watch and shaking Chay. But everything in between was a complete blank.

I thought slowly about this. I used my experience of hardship and lack of sleep and exertion to puzzle things out. I came up with the answer in the end. And it was a chilling one. Our lack of nutriment was dulling us. Our eyes and our ears and our minds were being dulled by the poorness of our food and the lack of fresh vitamins. We were slowly becoming robots tied to a computer programme which said: 'Two hours labour, two hours sleep, two hours labour, two hours sleep.'

Our minds may have been getting a little blank and

lethargic, but Chay was still filled for enthusiasm for adventure. Just before he and I had our evening meal—hot curry again—he started talking to me about the future.

'You know, Number One, this trip is soon going to be just a memory. I realise that it's a bit of a sweat and that we're getting a bit tired out, but you know and I know that we'll get there in the end. What are we going to do then? Do you think that there are other things we might do?'

This, of course, was a good point. What about the future—for up till then I had hardly dare think that there was a world outside the perpetual motion of 'Rosie'.

'What's your idea then?' I asked him.

'What about the Amazon? We've done a bit of canoe-ing in the past together. Don't you think we might be able to become the fastest people to canoe down the Amazon? I've read about head-hunters and Brazil nuts and savage jungles. I don't know anything about the land the river flows through. But I believe you and I could do it. We could manpack up over the Andes from Chile and then canoe down the Amazon.'

What about the Nile or the Great Lakes of Canada? What about the Rhine? These were thoughts I threw in. It is the original ideas that are hard to come by.

'No, the Nile and the Rhine are tame. No real adventure in the Rhine, for instance. You could stop every night at a pub and have a double feather bed each. That's not for us.

'The Great Lakes is not a bad idea. It's still wild there, and I've read about gales there where the water is as high as the Atlantic. That might do. But I would choose the Amazon.'

We talked about it for a while, and we finally left it at that—the Amazon or the Great Lakes.

Since we arrived home both Chay and I have rather gently hinted to our wives that sometime in the future we might take another trip if that was possible. We did not say anything definite and, after all, we had been away from the girls for a long time and had to be fairly considerate about ideas that might separate us again.

We made one mistake, however. Our daily logs had to be transcribed from the nearly illegible scribble of a blunt pencil in a notebook to the clearness of type-written entries. We thought we were the only people capable of dictating the logs to typists. We spent hours soon after we had arrived back dictating, with our wives by our sides.

My wife said, 'John, you're getting hoarse and so is Chay. Take a rest, go for a walk and Maureen and I will take over for a bit.'

So Chay and I went out for half an hour just to stretch our legs and get a breath of air. When we got back we told the girls we would take over again. They handed us our original logs and we began dictating again.

Marie-Christine came up to me after a minute or so and put her arms round my shoulders.

'John,' she said, 'if you want to go down the Amazon I shan't mind. I am behind you in anything you want to do. If it's the Amazon it's quite all right with me, so long as I'm included.'

Before I could reply to her Chay came in to our room from where he had been dictating next door. There was that quite irrepressible grin on his face.

'John, we made a big mistake. We left to go for our walk at exactly the wrong time when we were writing about the Amazon and the Great Lakes. I've been tackled on it and believe it or not it's on, so far as Maureen is concerned, providing we make it a four-some.'

I grinned back at Chay. 'I know. It seems to me that

these wives of ours have ganged up on us. M.C. says she wants to go too.'

But that was in the future, and we were still on the Atlantic with the winds keeping us from making ground towards home.

My log for Thursday, July 21 recorded our loneliness: 'We are very keen to see a ship, but they only seem to pass in the night.

'An eight-inch garfish found in the boat yesterday. I saw a lone tern again at night. Saw flying fish then dolphins and a large whale. Small fish (plankton?) very strongly for a few minutes at 16.00.

'This wind is very oppressive and we cannot get forward only N. very slowly. The rations situation is so very finely balanced that a week's delay will be most critical. We edge N. hoping to find W. wind with no success at all.'

Another incident that drew my mind back to the dangers of the sea happened during my second 'stag' that night of July 21. Again the lesson was driven home—the sea will have you the instant you relax.

I was rowing, Chay was asleep. I was determined to keep my mind on the job in hand. I did not want to lose another two hours as I had lost two earlier.

I put the oars in automatically for yet another stroke, an act that I had done God knows how many thousands of times before, when there was an extra jerk in my left arm and a shock in my left shoulder. I moved instinctively to massage my shoulder with my left hand—and the oar dropped out of the rowlock into the sea. One moment it was there, the next it was gone. The line had come undone.

I woke Chay. 'I've lost another oar. Keep your eyes skinned and see if we can spot it.'

I used the other oar to drive 'Rosie' round in a tight turn. We both looked. But the night was dark and the water looked even blacker. We could see nothing and we knew the oar could only be a few feet away from the side of the boat.

'It's no good, John, it's gone. I should carry on,' Chay said.

He was right again. Once a thing disappears over the side at night it has gone for ever. As I got another oar and settled down again I shuddered. What if Chay fell overboard during the night and knocked himself out? I would never find him. And how could I possibly go back and break the news to Maureen?

'Chay, are you asleep?' I called.

'No. What's up?'

'Please promise that you'll make certain that you wear your safety harness at all times when you're rowing alone at night. I was just having the shudders about what I'd say to Maureen if I didn't bring her husband back home to her.'

'Stop flapping. I've got some sea sense by now. Isn't my number Thirty-two? Anyway, John, this works both ways. You check on yours too. M.C. would kill me if I made it back alone. After all, she expects me to look after you.'

The next day I felt very depressed again, for the easterly winds continued. I just could not understand how for twenty-five per cent. of a month the winds could be directly contrary to what the weather charts say. I thought this was like a rabbit running up a wiremesh fence trying to find a hole so it could nip into the next field. The only difference was that the fence we were trying to cross was 40 degrees West. Once we were across that we would have crossed into our next field—the longitudes in the thirties. Thirty-nine West sounds much nearer to England than forty West.

Chay and I talked about this dreary and miserable fight against the easterlies, and we wondered whether we were being unsuccessful because we were in a poor shape. Lack of food was beginning to tell on us. I was sure. How could a man like myself, used to three good, solid meals a day, get by on 2,000 calories or less? It must have a grave effect over the weeks. The first effects were to depress us and to make every stroke a real effort.

This was the day when we changed our watches from Eastern Standard Time to Greenwich Mean Time. We put them on five hours. This takes a lot of getting used to. One moment it was breakfast time and the next it was after lunch. I thought that I might manage to get two meals in half an hour, but Chay dissuaded me. I was really feeling hungry all the time now, and two whacks of food would have made my day.

I awoke on July 23 feeling really worn out, as Chay and I had had only two spells of two hours' sleep during the night to make up for the change over to G.M.T. The first thing that upset me was the wind. It had changed all right—it had gone from South-east to North-east. We were now being blown South along the 40 West fence. That damned easterly, would it never switch to the West!

The day improved a bit later. First, I was cheered up by Chay's quoting to me the phrase of Mrs. Moore's, our friend back in the States.

'Above all, patience, John,' he told me. 'Do you remember that Mrs. Moore said that that would have to be our watchword. She was right.'

She was right. There was no point in getting bad tempered or impatient. You just had to take things as they come.

I was just thinking that Chay and I had spent fifty days in a boat with a living and rowing space of eight feet by four feet when I felt a slight fan of air. I waited again. And it came again. A breeze from the West.

'A westerly,' I said. 'Let's row a bit furiously and see if we can get across the fence.'

So we set to and really put our backs into it. We were finally making some progress, even though the wind was light, and we crossed the fence during the late evening. Thirty-nine West sounded very good to me.

Chay turned to me as he was making supper and said 'A week of this and we'll be Thirty West. Once we get there we will try out the Sarbe and see if we can raise a Shackleton. It would be good to have the R.A.F. overhead for a bit, and they'll be able to tell them at home where we are.'

This Sarbe beacon is a great set. It is a ground-to-air homing device which sends out an automatic signal on one of the R.A.F. frequencies and can be heard for probably fifty or sixty miles. We had been told before we left England to use it between 13.00 and 14.00 hours on Tuesdays and Thursdays once we got to Thirty West, for that was the longitude where British responsibility for the North Atlantic began. The set is only small, not much bigger than a cricket ball, and can be switched on or off. Many similar sets just keep sending signals until the batteries run out and are not much good when there is no battery shop down the road to refill them. So I agreed with Chay. To see an aircraft would really be great.

The next day the water was flat calm and looked as though it was sheeted in a tarnished steel. We rowed for twelve hours during the day. There was a little west wind, but it died down, and then we got a flukey wind from the North-east again. We just plodded and plodded in the hot sun. We were making progress, but at what a cost. We were both shattered, and when the night came we continued rowing together. I had never felt so tired in all my life. Chay reckoned that this day was the culminating point of the voyage.

training—running uphill at an Army training ground near Aldershot
part of our toughening-up programme (Chay Blyth on the left,
hn Ridgway right). Mock battles are fought here—for us, the real battle
s still a month away. We were fatter then!

English Rose III *is sheathed with nylon by an English firm. Left: This is her final protective coat*

Below: Almost ready for launching, the little boat is carried out from the boatyard

Right: The first trial run —English Rose III is launched down the slipway

Loading the polythene water bags which were stored under the floorboards of the boat to serve as ballast as well as drinking supplies

John Ridgway and Chay Blyth set out for a preliminary test row in English Rose III

Rough seas—when oars are shipped. The sea rages
as English Rose III *bobs on the edge of Hurricane Alma*

Calm seas—when John Ridgway went in to check if barnacles were attaching themselves to the boat

In mid-Atlantic.
This photograph of
English Rose III *on her*
voyage was taken by
a crewman of a ship
we met

Top left and right: Domestic scenes. Blyth, bearded, takes on a Viking look. We tried to shave regularly but it is difficult to use a razor in twenty-foot seas

Above: John Ridgway sleeping in the stern of English Rose III. We always woke cramped and cold—Chay said he felt like a human concertina

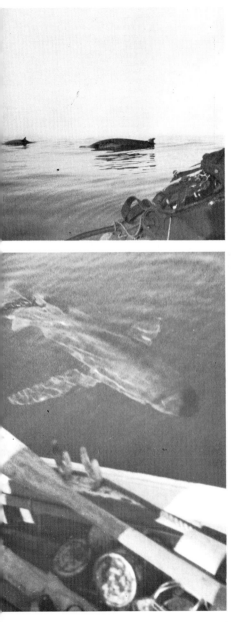

Top left: Curious whales bask beside English Rose III. One or two terrified us by diving beneath the tiny dory

Bottom left: Sharks, some of them huge, often accompanied the dory for long distances

Right: Birds were always a welcome sight. Their antics helped to relieve the monotony of rowing

Oarsman Blyth
—the only rowing he had ever done
before our tests in the Solent
was on the Serpentine in London's
Hyde Park

John Ridgway rows,
surrounded by a jumble of provisions.
Sometimes we could not completely
close our hands which had become
like claws

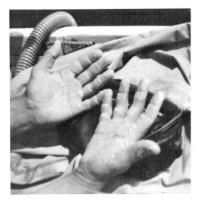

*John Ridgway's hands,
cracked and calloused from constant
hauling on the oars*

Waving goodbye to the Haustellum,
*after taking on the provisions
which saved us from starvation*

*How we attracted the attention of passing ships
—flying an anorak from our wireless aerial*

English Rose III's *little rudder guides her through the grey seas approaching Ireland*

'We must just stick it. Stick with it. That's what,' he kept saying like a litany in the background.

I got tired of agreeing with him and switched on our radio. They were playing Frank Sinatra's 'Strangers in the Night', and Sinatra was one of our favourites.

'Do you know what Frankie's doing now?' I asked Chay. 'He's just going out of his hotel suite in London, walking a few feet to a cocktail bar. Dry Martini first, then the head waiter takes the order for grub. I wonder what he eats?'

And later on: 'He's just taking a shower before turning in, in that enormous bed. Can you imagine the swishing of running water, thick white bath towels and the smell of a new bar of soap.'

We spent a long time discussing Frankie. We even sang some of his songs. I think it was Frankie who kept us sane on that never-ending day, but he could not get rid of our tiredness. We managed our first two hour watch each. When it came to my turn to do my second two-hour 'stag' I told Chay, 'I cannot do two hours. It'll kill me. Let's split the night into one-hour stints.'

I was a bit surprised when he agreed. I thought that he would insist on continuing. I had been prepared for an ironic 'What's wrong with you, are you cracking, or something?' For Chay to agree without argument was an even deeper depressive. If Chay feels the same as I do, then God help us, I thought.

We had just done too much in one day. We both decided that we must never over-exert ourselves again. As Chay pointed out, 'Suppose a sudden squall hit us—we'd never have the strength to fight it and we'd be lost without having a chance to do anything about it.'

We had forgotten the prime lesson. You must never give the sea a chance, otherwise it will kill you. I think that the sea must have been looking the other way that day, otherwise it could have had us without much trouble.

'I'm looking forward to finishing now,' wrote Chay. 'It's been a long time. Nothing but sea every day—we've only spoken to about five people since we started.

'We're not bored, as there is always something to do. Most of the time we can't find time to do it. We're not fed up with each other. We get on very well. We love this thing that if one is or feels sick or something the other always has that something to help the other along. We don't argue—both knowing the need for no clashes. We're always talking about something—all day and every day.

'We're a long way from giving up yet.'

On July 25, the next morning, we had a short conference. It was decided that we must catch up with some sleep if we were to keep going, so we curled up under the tarpaulin for two or three hours together. Then I continued to sleep while Chay did a 'stag'. He suddenly woke me up.

'John, John, quickly!' I woke up and heard this odd scraping noise. And then I felt 'Rosie' tilt.

'It's a shark, John,' Chay told me. We were both very worried. It was one thing to be capsized, but a different thing altogether to be capsized in the presence of a shark.

It was, in fact, rather wonderful to watch this shark. It was only about eight feet long and circled the boat just below the surface. He never went more than three or four yards away, then he would turn in towards us and scrape against the side. I grabbed a camera and took picture after picture. Once the shark came very close and its dorsal fin was within six inches of the boat. Chay grabbed it as it went by.

'It feels like leather. I should have hung on a bit, but I thought it might give a bit of a back flip. You don't want a one-handed man in the boat, do you?'

The shark swam around for about half an hour and we were entranced—until it started hitting the rudder quite hard. We could not let it damage 'Rosie', so we used a couple of spinners on our lines to try and frighten it away. But it was not interested. I got out a tin of shark repellent—not that I thought it would do much good. I was very surprised when the creature suddenly gave a flip of its tail and fled about three minutes after I had emptied the tin into the water. It was good to know that we were able to scare sharks off if we had to.

We saw many birds during these two tranquil days, and I sketched some of them in my log book—terns, Mother Carey's chickens, brown gulls, black cap gulls and small billed mottled gulls with thick heads. In the gloriously calm evening we saw several dolphins; they approached the groups of gulls in the water and seemed to play with them. The gulls did not seem to mind the surfacing fish except to unfold their wings. There cannot have been many spectators like us, I reflected—man is usually a fleeting passer-by on the ocean, and the view from a rowing boat is very different to that from a steamer.

By that night we were much rested. We had our usual supper of curry and we were both new men. I was rowing just before midnight. It was a still, black night and Chay was asleep. I was lulled by the unending monotony. It was an idyllic night.

I was shocked to full wakefulness by a swishing noise to starboard. I looked out into the water and suddenly saw the writhing, twisting shape of a great creature. It was outlined by the phosphorescence in the sea as if a string of neon lights were hanging from it.

It was an enormous size, some thirty-five or more feet long, and it came towards me quite fast. I must have watched it for some ten seconds. It headed straight at me and disappeared right beneath me.

I stopped rowing. I was frozen with terror at this apparition. I forced myself to turn my head to look over the port side. I saw nothing, but after a brief pause I heard a most tremendous splash.

I thought that this might be the head of the monster crashing into the sea after coming up for a brief look at us. I did not see the surfacing—just heard it.

I am not an imaginative man, and I searched for a rational explanation for this incredible occurrence in the night as I picked up the oars and started rowing again. Chay and I had seen whales and sharks, dolphins and porpoises, flying fish—all sorts of sea creatures but this monster in the night was none of these. I reluctantly had to believe that there was only one thing it could have been—a sea serpent.

I could understand now the tales of the ancient mariners. I had seen what they had. And like them, the memory of that incredible creature will stay with me for the rest of my life.

I told Chay about it when he woke up. I thought he would say that I had been seeing things and I was relieved when he just said simply, 'I believe you, John. This is a very strange ocean. I'm not surprised at anything.'

We both had a good night's sleep and awoke refreshed to fight yet another south-easterly breeze on July 26. We rowed but made little headway. We saw four ships in twelve hours that day and fired flare after flare at them. One passed about a mile away, and yet despite the brightness of the red mini-flares that Chay and I lit, it just kept on its way. I am surprised at the very poor lookout kept by many of these merchantmen. Supposing we had been dying when we used our flares? No one seemed to be keeping their eyes open.

A little later, of course, I had to change my mind. A ship seemed to be coming straight towards us—it passed only a few hundred yards away and luckily saw our frantic waving. It was the *Madaket* bound for New York. They asked us if we wanted any stores or water, and we turned both offers down.

I was interested in getting a position from them. '46 degrees 56 minutes North, 37 degrees 39 minutes West,' an officer on the bridge shouted down to us. We had not spoken to a ship for twenty-seven days.

I went over the moon. For that was almost exactly the position that I had worked out. My navigation was bang on and, as Chay said, we were really independent of navigational assistance from anyone. We could cope with anything.

We waved at the *Madaket,* got the oars out again and started off. As the *Madaket* got under way again she gave us a blast on her siren. It was a sad sound and a sad sight to watch the ship with its kindliness disappear into the evening.

Nightmare

Chay Blyth: July 27–August 4

> *Where lies the land to which the ship would go?*
> *Far, far ahead, is all her seamen know.*
> *And where the land she travels from? Away,*
> *Far, far behind, is all that they can say.*

THE words of Arthur Clough's poem describe rather well my feelings as I squatted over the radio during the lonely pre-dawn 'stag'. We were almost halfway across and at our furthest point from land. Had we left the worst dangers behind us, or had they been just a taste of the real terrors still to come, I wondered.

Suddenly through the whistling atmospherics coming from the radio I heard my own name being mentioned. The *Madaket* had reported our position, and from a warm studio somewhere in London the B.B.C. announcer was advising the world that Paratroopers Ridgway and Blyth were safe and well. This meant that Lloyd's had our position, and probably in just a few hours Captain Thomson would be telephoning the news to our wives.

I tried to imagine Maureen's reaction. She was with her mother in Newcastle. Would she laugh or cry when Colin told her? I remembered the way she had clung to me that day we left England to fly to America. I had tried to comfort her and reassure her, but I sensed she felt she was saying goodbye to me for the last time.

Thank God she had never been to sea, and so at least

could be spared from knowing just what the conditions were like out there. The B.B.C. announcer went on to discuss the new political moves taking place in Rhodesia, and I cut him off in mid-sentence with a flick of the switch.

It was a wonderful clear night with just the faintest hint of a breeze from the South-east. There was not a single cloud in the sky to mar the star-speckled dome, and I could clearly see to the horizon. Only the sound of John's breathing and the slight hiss of water along the sides broke the silence, and it was difficult to believe that nearly a thousand miles to the South a hurricane was rushing towards us with the speed of a London–Edinburgh express.

By the end of my 'stag' the breeze had freshened to a steady wind, and when John next woke me to replace him at the oars a big sea was running and I had to shout to make myself heard above the noise of wind and waves.

John pointed to the sky. Heavy black clouds were racing low overhead, and I felt the first big spots of rain on my face.

'I don't think I've made any headway at all in the last hour,' John bellowed in my ear. 'If anything, I've been losing ground.'

'Well, let me give it a try,' I shouted back. 'The wind's pretty strong, so perhaps the storm will blow over quickly.'

He shrugged his shoulders and crawled under the canvas. I did not really believe the storm would pass over quickly, but hated to admit right at the start that my two hours' slogging at the oars was not going to carry us more than a few yards nearer home. It was depressing to work so hard and know that gradually, hour by hour, the sea was pressing us back to the West.

The slamming jar of the waves on the end of the oars

at the start of every stroke had an accumulative effect on both mind and body when the wind was in the East. It was a form of punch drunkenness. I found I could sit there for an hour without a single thought in my head, and be so little aware of the soreness of my hands that my arms might have been ten yards long.

At those times the brain worked slowly, but the imagination was a vivid thing, and I terrified myself with thoughts of primeval creatures rising from the incredible depths to seize and destroy our boat. When in this condition neither of us wanted our food. The pummelling from the oars combined with fear and tiredness to kill our appetites.

That day marked the beginning of a new phase in our voyage. Far from passing over quickly, the storm lasted for nearly a week. For three days and nights we were unable to row and unable to sleep. We had both known fear many times before in our lives—but never anything like this. The sea was like something out of hell. Lacking keel, sail or motor, we could not keep 'Rosie's' head into the sea, and she thrashed piteously like a mad dog in convulsions. We knew that this could not be over tomorrow, or for many tomorrows. It was like being rubbed down with rough sandpaper.

By then we had lost track of how many storms there had been, knowing only that each one left us progressively weaker and one step nearer defeat. At 2 p.m. on July 27 we shipped oars and hauled the mildewed canvas canopy into place on its metal frame. There was no longer any use trying to disguise the fact that we were running into trouble.

The situation was already serious. That morning while trying to pick up a B.B.C. news bulletin a freak wave had broken right over the boat and swamped our radio. We tried to persuade ourselves that it had only been temporarily put out of action. But neither of us really believed this.

'Perhaps when it's had a chance to dry out it will be all right,' said John. 'The water has probably got to the points and it is shorting out.'

'And if it doesn't work?'

'Then we'll just have to rely on the watches to time our sighting,' he said. 'I expect they're pretty accurate. And if they're not there's damn all we can do about it now.'

Until then we had been able to check and reset the watches by the radio time signals. They had never been more than a few seconds out. But in three weeks those seconds could mount up and eventually cause a serious error in calculating our position.

Our log notes were running to double the length of previous entries. We scribbled away in the hope that by writing down our problems we would unload some of the worry.

On Thursday, July 28 John wrote: 'As darkness falls it is apparent that we are unable to row any longer, as each change-over between men entails a swing off course, and the energy required to bring her back is too much.

'All the time we are slowly slipping back. As we eat our curry and drink our cocoa we decide to slip the sea anchor.... We have been almost stationary for so long there are several small fishes under the boat, and as I put the sea anchor over Blyth tries to sniggle one in best Scottish fashion. The fish is about eight inches long and fairly deep and mottled brown and white in colour.

'We didn't catch it. Neither of us wanted our food. This was caused in me by an amalgamation of pure fear and seasickness. We now realise our position and are both simply afraid. With the sea anchor over we both curl up under the canopy in the stern—both wet before it started. The salt is extremely irritating to our skin, and the position very cramped and a nightmare for anyone who suffers from claustrophobia. A grim, grim day.'

My own log was equally stark. 'We have been rowing against this south-east wind now for three days,' I wrote. 'Now we've reduced it to one hour on and one hour sleeping. My hands are very sore indeed. I can't clench my fists. It seems all the tendons and muscles in all my fingers have been pulled. Before I start my hour's sleep I put lanoline on my hands, but they are so painful it doesn't seem to help. When I wake up it's a nightmare those first few minutes. My hands won't do anything. When you take a stroke you get this fantastic jerk on your arms and hands. How I pray the wind will change to the West.

'There's been some fish following us all day. When we throw some paper over the side they dart out to it and then back to the stern. We rowed all day and then the seas gradually built up. At 10.00 G.M.T. it was getting dark and the seas were very large by this time. We decided to put over the sea anchor. The first time for over a month or more—I can't really remember. The night was spent in the two sleeping positions. Very uncomfortable and not a great deal of sleep. I got soaked all down my legs and behind. The water rushed in under the canopy into my boots and down my trouser leg. This only happened once, but it was enough.

'We used water-bags inflated as pillows and to put next to us where something would be sticking into us. I slept next to the pumps, but was very lucky. I only had to get up four times to pump out. I only hope the sea anchor holds the night.'

On July 29 we emerged only once from beneath the canvas canopy, and that was to check the sea anchor. To have lost it at that point would have been a disaster. For nothing could have stopped us being blown West with the wind, and we could easily have lost fifty miles.

We spent the day huddled together in the stern in a space measuring no more than five feet by four feet. John felt very sick and tried to sleep as much as possible.

The waves were like mountains and bigger than any we had seen up till then. Their tops were sliced flat by the wind, and they came towards us frighteningly fast and with a noise like a plane on full throttle. We learned to judge by their speed and sound which waves were going to pass under us, which would break into the boat and which would hit us smack on.

The constant battering of hundreds of pounds of falling water on the canvas canopy finally proved too much for the metal frame. It collapsed and introduced yet another form of personal discomfort. We tried to prop the edges up with two stout poles from our emergency kit. Every half minute or so the wind would lift the canvas. The poles would dislodge and the whole soggy mess would come tumbling down on our heads. We were driven almost to the point of hysteria.

Again I think it is worthwhile quoting from our logs to explain the full misery of that day. Nothing I can add now would so completely capture the events and feelings we experienced.

Wrote John: 'The sea anchor seems to hold well—I believe because it does not have a rigid ring at the mouth, but can "breathe" like a parachute.

'As night draws on we think of Samuelson and Harbo and how they rowed into a great easterly wind for two days and then lay exhausted at sea anchor—an exact parallel to our present circumstances. On the third night they were overturned. We believe *English Rose III* to be more seaworthy.

'Tonight we lie and wait—nothing could save us if we get into difficulties. No ship could get us off these seas, even if it arrived in time. We are completely in God's hands, at the mercy of the weather. All night the wind screams louder and louder and the sound of the sea becomes louder. We talked of many things, the night train to Scotland, the things we had done. And slowly we were overtaken by an enormous feeling of humility and the desire to return and try to live a better life.'

I noted a similar conclusion in my own log.

'We stayed in our beds all day. You really start thinking of the good things in your life. A lot of humble pie can easily be eaten in a situation like this. There's only one word for it—nightmare.

'We often think of Johnstone and where he is. How fortunate for him he has a cabin. If both boats make this I'll shake his hand. If he's having it the same as us, as he must, he's having it rough. We ate very little. No hot meals. We would have had to move everything to cook. The best way round this is to sleep. The sticks that kept the canopy up kept falling down. The wind would lift it a little and it would come down and hit us on the head about five times a minute. It would drive you to the point of getting angry—which I did. About 18.00 I got up to check the sea anchor. Okay. Pump out. I looked at the waves. They were huge. The biggest we've had so far. This must surely be the effect of the hurricane. It was almost white everywhere I looked.

'At 3.00 hours we were wakened by the storm. The wind howled and the waves crashed against the stern and bow. Whack! It would hit the boat—but "Rosie" took it all. What a boat this is, wonderful. The dorymen certainly knew what they were talking about.

'I pumped out very few times. Awful.

'You could hear the waves roar like an engine coming towards you, crash into you, then roar off into the night. Then the next one. Only one thing for it. Sleep then prayer. God comes close to you out here.

'You have three feet on each side of you. Then death.

'I have never been so frightened before as I am here. I pray tomorrow that it will change. During the night I get fantastic pains in the knees. It came from them being bent for so long.

'We are now both sleeping on the side which is away from the wind so that the side nearest the wind is higher and helps stop the water coming over the side.

'My feet are numb. This must be the effect of the cold and the canopy resting on top of them. This canopy is continually wet now, laying on top of me. I can't get away from it.'

The Lord must have heard our prayers, for early the next morning—Saturday, July 30—the wind shifted to the North-west. We hauled in the sea anchor, and with the waves decreasing by the minute, we were soon racing eastwards with John on the oars.

But the sea had not finished with us yet. As the afternoon dragged past the wind swung round to the South, and by early evening we were in the grip of another storm, having had no chance to dry out and still reeling from tiredness and exposure.

The seas rapidly climbed to enormous proportions and life became a constant nightmare once more. For John the suffering was even more intense. He had developed a rash from knees to hips, and his neck was circled with salt water sores. The only thing in our first aid kit which gave him any relief at all was foot powder —and we were already down to our last tin.

During the night it began to rain and the winds grew even fiercer. Dawn found us weakening rapidly and almost crying from lack of sleep. We were weary now to be finished, but home seemed so far away. There was a growing desperation in both of us to put an end to it— but that we were unable to do.

For four days we had been soaked to the skin. The salt water worked its way into our sores and John's rash, and every movement meant further pain and misery.

Again the wind veered round to the West, but the storm continued without a let-up, and we saw nature performing tricks which defy logic. Great mountains, covered in icing sugar, marched endlessly towards the East, and we, thank God, were dragged along with them.

It is difficult to say which was worst, being on or off watch. The choice: to crouch soaking wet under a pile of streaming canvas or sit in the open wrapped in a dripping blanket. John looked exhausted with dark, sunken eyes, and I dreaded to think how I must look.

So we crashed on and on. Nothing mattered but to keep on going. 'Rosie' seemed like a thing alive. We hung precariously for long moments, balancing on the crest of a wave, surfing eastward with a speed that was terrifying yet wonderful. The dory took a terrible battering—but seemed to be indestructible. This fight against nature was going the whole distance, with only one round to the elements. A small hand-painted plaque was ripped from our stern.

It had been fastened there by George Hitchcock, a Cape Codder who gave us tremendous assistance in preparing for the crossing.

It was while I was out with George, taking lessons in rowing, that it suddenly dawned on me just what we were attempting. I turned to him and said, 'Three thousand miles. What the hell have I done?'

He had scored these words on the plaque along with another quote: 'Let's get bloody rowing.' It was a phrase we used often in the days preceding our departure from Cape Cod.

'Let's get bloody rowing,' we said, 'and get on with the job.'

I missed that tiny plaque, that and a nine-year-old letter from my mother and the last letter from Maureen were very comforting in moments of strain. Also the verse which the dorymen put on one of the watertight compartment doors:

> *When at last I sight the shore,*
> *And the fearful breakers roar,*
> *Fear not, He will pilot me.*

This I believed in.

We were both certain by now that we were going to make it, providing our food and water lasted out. The most important question, and one which we spent hours discussing, was how much longer we would be at sea.

There was no longer any question of our reaching England by mid-August. Our planned progress of a degree a day had become something of a poor joke. The aim now was to make landfall by September 1, and we believed this was still possible, despite the delays caused by the storm.

We wanted to be there in time to enjoy the last few weeks of summer. I promised myself a quiet week's holiday with my wife. Then up to Hawick for a week's fishing. From there I planned to join John and his wife at their croft in Sutherland.

Normally I would have been starting my annual leave on August 1. Before I learned about John's proposed rowing of the Atlantic Maureen and I had planned a holiday in Greece. It was to have been a camping holiday lasting a month, and a friend from my unit and his fiancée were going with us. But I had no regrets. I had known just what I was taking on when I made my offer to John. The Greek islands I could visit another year, but rowing the Atlantic was a once in a lifetime chance.

Tuesday, August 2. We hoped the R.A.F. rescue Shackleton would make another attempt to find us that day. But we were too tired and the sea was too rough to try the Sarbe beacon. Conditions on that day at least were very much against the R.A.F.

'It was very cloudy and the sun didn't come through at all,' I wrote in my log. 'Another day and we are still wet. Our feet are cold now. We must be getting near England. We're pretty "gunjy" now as well. What I'd give for a shower and clean kit! I'm looking forward to the day when we have our shave. I think the test has really started now. Each day we're out it gets just that little bit harder. There is not so much sun, therefore we do not get dry. This means rowing for longer periods in wet kit.'

That evening we saw a tanker. We had just a fleeting glimpse of it as it steamed out of the gloom before it vanished again heading in the direction of America. It could not have known we were there. At least it gave no sign of having seen us and we did not have time to fire a flare. We also saw several birds, including a black capped tern which almost landed on John's head.

The wind continued to blow strongly, no longer at gale force, but powerfully enough to halt our progress when it shifted round once more to the East. That delay lasted twelve hours, and for once we were not too upset by it. We slept the sleep of utter exhaustion and woke after ten hours to find the wind had dropped and was from the South-west.

I wrote: 'We went with the wind all day, one man rowing while the other washed and shaved. I feel better for a shave. Our kit is quite dirty now, caked with green mildew from the canvas. But we cannot spare the water to wash our outer clothes. In sea-water the dirt just doesn't come out. It's only the clothes directly in contact with the skin—underpants, vests and socks—that we wash.'

Our washing procedure was always the same: first soak in sea-water, then wring out and wash with soap in fresh water. Rinse in sea-water and wring out, then rinse in fresh water and wring out.

Our outer clothes were beginning to show definite signs of wear, and we had sealed several splits with black masking tape. But as for washing them—that would have to come later.

Hunger

John Ridgway: August 5–13

ON August 5 I wrote in my log: 'It is hard to describe how depressing it is to row all day head into the wind when you are a thousand miles from home, knowing full well that at the end of the day after all the toil you are still a thousand miles from home.'

The biting easterly winds with icy rain had returned and, with each oar stroke which pushed us forward, I felt that we were really sliding back towards America. The cruelty of the situation for the first time brought on pangs of self-pity, and there were moments when both of us could have broken down. For two months we had strained day and night, every nerve and muscle in our bodies stretched to breaking-point; I began to feel we were fading.

This was largely a mental condition brought on by the never-ending frustrations, the discomfort, the always-wet clothes and the salt water that burnt into the skin like acid. God, how I began to hate that sea-water. Our faces, hands and arms were reddened and sore, and boils caused spears of stabbing pain all over our bodies. It was difficult enough to row, but to bring one's whole body into contact with rough surfaces when trying to sleep was an agony that was fast becoming unbearable.

Low rations had taken us on to the verge of starvation, and daily I could see that Chay was losing weight. His normally round, chubby features were sunken and there were dark rings beneath his eyes. I felt sorry for

Chay. Although he had been a willing partner on the enterprise from the very beginning, I somehow felt responsible for bringing him, and when the darkest thoughts of surviving went through my mind I hoped that he, at least, would be saved.

Our spirits were low and Chay's old bursts of humour were rare. He had kept the boat alive. Now he was silently grim, and I felt that whatever was left in him was ebbing fast. The thought frightened and shocked me. I would not know what to do without him. I was quite sure that if only one of us was capable of rowing we should never make it.

Previously, when we sighted a ship, however far out on the horizon it might be, Chay would grip my arm and yell, 'Look, a ship! I wonder if it will come our way?' Then one of us would zip our anorak to an oar, with the blade in the hood, and wave it slowly back and forth in an attempt to attract attention. Once Chay's anorak fell in the sea, but we managed to retrieve it.

I had always experienced the greatest exultation from testing myself to the limit. Climbing hills with a fifty-pound pack, canoeing for twenty hours on end and driving myself to a state of exhaustion gave me a kind of pride that my body could stand so much, and I suppose that was one of the underlying motives of rowing the Atlantic.

At first it was interesting to examine the effect of gradually running ourselves down, and we were determined to survive on whatever we had on board. When early on in the voyage ships stopped and gave us our position we always declined offers of food. We even refused cups of coffee.

Now I had an agonising re-appraisal. I realised I was wrong in turning down offers of food and stores from the *Madaket*, the ship we had met only a few days before.

I regretted our stupid obstinacy, because our rapid deterioration could have brought us to the point when we should seriously have had to consider tugging the red handle of our emergency transmitter. An S.O.S. would have brought ships and aircraft to our aid, and lives might be lost in the process.

This was something we could not allow to happen. I talked it over at some length with Chay on a blustery day when our progress was nil. We rowed steadily just to prevent us being blown backwards.

'When we started out,' I called, 'we made up our minds to go all the way without help from anybody. What do you feel about that now, Chay?'

Chay paused for a moment, his head hung down. He seemed to have great difficulty in replying.

'Maybe what you want me to say is that we should carry on as we are and hope for the best,' he said after a moment or two. 'But I'm not going to say that. I'm going to say that we'd be mad not to stop the first ship we see and ask them for some grub. We are not going to lose anything by doing that. But it could be the difference between life and death—and I think I'm too young to die. How about you?'

'I'm glad you said that,' I replied. 'I've been wondering whether it was going chicken to beg a little help. I realise now, of course, it won't be. I agree with you— let's get help from the first ship that sees us.'

I felt a lot better after that. I knew that, having made the decision, there was absolutely nothing more that we could do. It was a position in which I could find, strange as it may seem, a little satisfaction.

I am not a nerveless person. I am very conscious of fear. I am frightened of parachuting. I don't like doing it at all. But when I am faced with really acute danger I am able to stop worrying and to relax and rather enjoy it. I know that I have done all I can to help myself and the situation is out of my hands. I like the situation to build to the point where I cannot make any more decisions, to get past the stage where I am responsible, so there is nothing else to do but to sit back and try to enjoy it.

It was a state of mind I tried hard to create at that stage of the trip. I wanted to keep happy and let the body take care of itself. I am not sure that I succeeded, for the body could never take care of itself. It had to be nourished, and daily the physical attack, which was so marked at the beginning of the trip, lessened. Slowly but surely malnutrition was gripping our bodies and hunger pains began to build up, especially after eating a meal which was quite inadequate for our needs. Our main meal of the day was in the evening, curry and rice, always curry and rice, and we ate with our communal wooden spoon from the pressure cooker in which the food had been prepared.

Our rule was that whoever rowed the first night 'stag' would eat last. This led to a fine point of etiquette following a slight difference of opinion one night when I accused Chay of eating a bit more than his fair share.

He had eaten seven spoonfuls and a bit, whereas when it came to my turn there was only sufficient for six spoonfuls, plus the scrapings around the inside of the cooker. When I pointed this out to Chay, he said, 'But I take smaller amounts on the spoon than you. If you did the same you would also have seven spoonfuls.'

'I don't agree with you,' I said. 'Both of us are so very hungry we pile as much on to the spoon as we can.'·

On reflection, it was rather a trivial and childish dispute, but it had to be resolved, and we did this in the following way. We agreed that we would take the first night 'stag' alternately—which meant to say that we would take it in turns at supper-time to eat last. And we agreed that whoever ate first would consume fractionally less than his fair share to make certain the other man got his full ration before going on duty. By the end of the trip we had got this down to a fine art, and I doubt if there was more than a quarter of a teaspoonful difference between our respective rations.

The hunger pains got worse, and we tried a kind of self-hypnosis to retard our mental state. We thought if we tried to think of nothing the senses would be numbed to the pains. This produced a kind of super 'mental plonk', and I began to dream even when I was awake. My mind produced the most superb fantasies, so that as I rowed I would see pictures in the sky and in the water.

My mind, too, would relive episodes from my schooldays. I would be fishing with my friends in a narrow stream, three or four miles from Pangbourne Nautical College, Berkshire, and would walk back in the dusk, watching the smoke stream lazily from the chimneys of the old houses near Tidmarsh. It would rise straight into the wintry air. All was warm and secure, and soon we would be back at college, ready for an evening meal. The scream of a bird, perhaps, would return me to the realities of the present. It was a harsh contrast.

My state of mind was such that I imagined a seagull was perching on my head. I saw it fly towards the boat, swoop, settle for a moment on the gunwales, then hop on to my head. 'That's funny,' I said to Chay. 'I had the feeling there was a seagull on my head. I could feel it. I'm sure if I put my hand up I could touch it.'

Chay turned and whispered, 'There *is* a seagull on your head. A real one.' My whole body shivered with fear. I lifted the oars from the water and put them inboard. I sat still without moving a muscle. I felt sick. And I simply could not raise an arm to shoo it away. It remained on my head for about forty-five seconds before it took off and flew away into the gloom.

It left me feeling quite ill with fright. I thought it to be an omen of some kind, and I felt it might be a messenger sent to single me out for something.

I wrote in my log—somewhat theatrically now that I look back: 'Was that sea-bird on my head the clutch of doom, I wonder? There are so many things I want to do, to try to make those around me a little happier. Surely this cannot be the end so soon?'

I was so sure that something was going to happen to me that I kept my twenty-foot nylon safety line fastened for the rest of the day.

Suddenly, about six-thirty in the evening, soon after the bird had flown away, Chay gave a shout. 'There's a ship!' I looked in the direction to which he pointed and, sure enough, I saw a big cargo ship, only about a thousand yards away.

Holding on to each other to steady ourselves as the boat bobbed from side to side in the high running seas, we raised an oar with an anorak tied to the end like a flag and waved it between us. We shouted and did everything we could to make those in the ship see us. It was our one big chance to restock with food. We *must* stop it somehow.

I am sure there were tears in our eyes as we shouted frantically, 'Hey there. Hey there,' but our voices were lost on the wind.

'Quick,' I said. 'Get the flare signals. They are bound to see those.'

I grabbed one of the three precious flares left, aimed at the ship and fired. The flare shot through the air, a long line of smoke trailing behind it. But it dropped short, and we both looked at each other and said, 'Blast—still, they might have seen it.'

But those on the ship apparently did not see it, for it

just sailed past us, its majestic shape outlined against the skyline. We watched it go off into the distance without saying another word.

As it disappeared out of sight, Chay just looked at me, shrugged and said, 'Well—would you credit that!'

I could not think of anything to say. I turned and carried on with the mechanical task of pumping, which, in our condition, was becoming more and more of an effort.

We had been shipping quite a lot of water while trying to stop the ship, and when we got back to work we found it was nearly a foot deep in the bottom of the boat. The small compass, pieces of string, pencils, a jersey, were all afloat. It all looked a horrible mess and made us feel even more sorry for ourselves.

A strong east and north-easterly wind kept up all day, and the waves were really high. It was still a fight to prevent being blown westwards, but it was not possible for both of us to row at once because of the heavy seas which kept sweeping over us and filling the boat. At eight o'clock in the evening, as we were preparing our evening meal, half a meat block, half a packet of diced mixed vegetables and a cup of cocoa, we nearly lost the lot when another wave swamped us.

Chay saw it coming. It rose higher and higher as it drew near to us, and we sat watching it and bracing ourselves for the impact. Suddenly Chay remembered our dinner in the cooker—and just managed to slam the lid on in time as the huge wave struck us. After our meagre meal, we had another spell of bailing and pumping out, although we knew we were in for a night of it as the wind increased and the sea grew wilder.

Each wave was like a train as it approached us—not a train going non-stop but one that pauses and then continues and pauses again. The roar comes when the wave breaks. But a wave at sea doesn't just break and disappear the way it does when it hits the shore. At sea the water tumbles down into the trough, and then the wave picks itself up again and comes on silently. Then you hear it crash near by and you know the next time it is going to hit you. We had some waves break right over the boat, but it was extraordinary the way the dory seemed to get up on the wave so that it actually broke beneath us and we would be skipping along on a swirl of white foam.

I have always had tremendous respect for water. It is the enormous power of it, not only of the sea but of an ordinary stretch of river. At my croft in Scotland, where I often go for my leave, even on a calm day it is deeply impressive to see the Atlantic hitting the rocks, to see the way the water drops back from the cliffs and then sucks it up again, the enormous, unharnessed power of it. I find water deeply moving. I do not know why this is—perhaps because I am English. I do not think I am afraid of water, but anyone who feels this way about something has to go out and challenge it.

But on that day, August 5, the day the gull landed on my head, the day the ship which was so near passed us, that day of the most appalling winds and seas, it was a battle I was not sure we were winning.

In my log I wrote: 'Somehow there must be a way out of this trap. We are now eating on a survival basis, rather than a working basis, so we are caught between two stools, as we can't fight east wind ... this depression and self-pity is an interesting and anticipated phase of this experience. The shortage of rations and slowness of progress is not.'

After eating our meal that night, Chay took the first 'stag' from 11 to 1 a.m., while I crawled beneath the canopy, wrapped myself in the wet blanket and tried to doze off. I could feel the pains returning in my stomach, and I tried to blank my mind from them and think about something else.

I gave this up after a while. I kept thinking of food, and my imagination roamed over the most succulent dishes I had ever eaten. I imagined great plates of thickly cut roast beef, fried prawns, lobster thermidor and huge cuts of the finest fillet steak. My mouth watered.

Suddenly I decided to pray, an earnest prayer which I hoped would mean more than the other prayers I had said at difficult times during the voyage. I have never been a regular churchgoer, and prayer has always been regarded by me as an expedient in an emergency. I had never honestly considered that anybody would bother to listen to any prayer that I said. On the night of August 5 I said my prayers at length, forcing my swollen fingers straight by pressing my hands together in the attitude I had been taught as a child. Indeed, I repeated this action every remaining night of the voyage and I felt a union with God that I had never before experienced. When I finished I poked my head from beneath the canvas and looked up at the clouds. From that moment I was convinced that we were being looked after and that a ship would come along with provisions before the last of our rations ran out.

At 1 a.m. I changed over with Chay, soon after he spotted another ship to the North bound for Europe. In the darkness it was impossible to do anything to try to stop it.

'Never mind, Chay,' I said. 'I'm sure a ship will turn up soon.'

'I've been praying for that for days,' he replied, 'and nothing's happened yet.'

'It will,' I said. We were approaching the South American lane.

For the next two hours I pulled at the oars and felt

that we were making a little progress, however small, through the night, then handed back to Chay, who emerged from the canopy rubbing his eyes and saying, 'I've had an odd sort of dream. I can't remember what it was. I've got a feeling something is going to happen. It's either going to be a ship or a really bad storm.'

I hate premonitions, and I wished Chay had not reminded me in an indirect way about the gull, which I still regarded as a bad omen. I crawled into our little canvas shelter and hoped that this time I would have better luck getting some sleep.

I had been there about forty minutes and had just dozed off when I heard shouts from Chay. 'Get up quickly and put your harness on. We could be overturned here ...' I crawled out and asked him what was the matter.

'Look at those,' he said, pointing to two huge whales in the water outlined by the moonlight. They were just about the biggest we had seen since we started and were a magnificent, frightening sight as they cruised first one way and then the other.

Suddenly one of them came towards us like a submarine just below the surface. You could see the top of his huge black head and his massive tail swishing about forty feet behind. It came closer to us, and we both just sat there, watching them, patiently waiting for 'Rosie' to rise and—we hoped—slide off its massive back. But, twenty feet away, it turned swiftly and joined its partner, which was blowing like a steam gusher a couple of hundred yards away. Thankful that the danger had passed, I returned to try to sleep, only to be awakened again by Chay's shouts five minutes later.

'Quick—come out,' he shouted again. I scrambled out and joined him. He pointed once again to the two massive shapes of the whales which had returned—this time to make a closer inspection of us and our boat. The nearest whale came to about fifteen yards away. I could see the moonlight glinting on its pig-like eyes.

Chay and I sat there petrified. We did not know whether to shout and make a noise or to keep quiet. The sea was somewhat calmer, and the two great mammals rose and fell like submarines, their huge tail fins flapping and making a noise like the breeze catching a collapsing tent.

We decided to keep quiet and see what happened, knowing that just one flick from those powerful tails might splinter us into destruction. Suddenly they both 'let off steam' and huge fountains of water shot into the air. We quaked, watching paralysed as the whales slithered below the surface and reappeared the same distance away to port.

Quietly, I said to Chay, 'Get the flash-lamp.'

'If you shine that at them they'll only come closer,' he replied.

'Let's take a chance,' I said. 'I think they might be scared off by the sudden light shining at them.'

Chay produced the lamp and aimed it in the direction of the whales, which moved smoothly, but far too slowly for my liking, past us, seeming to eye us as if making up their minds whether to let us alone or turn us over.

The lamp was switched on, then off. In that brief moment I could see by the powerful beam the black oily-looking skin of one of the whales.

Chay switched the lamp on again, and to my horror I saw a whale coming straight for us. Chay kept the lamp on this time and directed it at the monster's huge square head, which suddenly dipped and the whale disappeared with a terrific thwack of the tail striking the surface of the water. It must be coming directly beneath the boat, I thought, and looked round wildly for our life-jackets, at the same time trying to remember what I had read in

boyhood stories about the fate of men swallowed whole
by such creatures.

The sea around the boat heaved as the whale made its
way below the surface to join its mate, which had now
moved to a position to starboard. We expected at any
moment to feel the boat being lifted in the air, if the
whale had not gone deep enough, or chose to surface
again immediately below us. The whale reappeared beside its mate, and both moved off into the night with
great splashes as they cavorted, snorted and blew water
high into the air.

It was an unnerving ordeal, and Chay and I stayed
together talking for some time after they left. To calm
ourselves we opened a tube of Smarties and ate the lot
between us—on consideration, a rather rash form of self-
generosity with our provisions so low. There was only
one tube each per week.

The following day we again took stock of our clothing, which was full of holes and rotting from exposure to
the salt sea and air. Thick crusts of salt had formed
round the cuffs and neckbands of track suits and jerseys,
causing the most painful chafing. Although we kept
rinsing these parts, they quickly formed again and were
eating into the material, which began to disintegrate.

I wrote in my log that day: 'Depression seems to tie
my empty stomach in knots. We are both filled with re-
morse over the worry we are causing our wives....'

Our great ambition was to get past 20 degrees West,
which would place us only six hundred miles from the
British Isles. At that time, Saturday, August 6, we were
still about a thousand miles from home and had only
enough food to last us twenty-eight days. The need to
see a ship became an obsession, and daily we scanned the
horizon. We saw several, but, despite our frantic waving,
all of them passed by without seeing us. Some were not
so far away—about a mile—and the fact that they did not

see us brought home to us how small we were and that we would have to almost be run down before we were spotted.

As much as we wanted to meet a ship, the thought of being run down was always uppermost in our minds throughout the whole of the trip, especially at night, when we would be impossible to see. Sometimes at night a ship would pass close enough for us to hear its engines, and once in fog we had the most terrible fright.

We heard its engines softly at first. Then they grew steadily louder. We could hear plainly the thump-thump-thump of the diesels. As the ship drew closer, we could hear the great rush of it through the water. But we could not tell which direction it was coming from— there were no lights and the sound enveloped us in the fog. I blew our pitifully small fog-horn a couple of times and then gave up. We just sat there, staring wildly around us and waiting to be destroyed. Then the thing roared past us, still without showing any lights, and the thump-thump-thump receded. We slumped back in relief as the swells from the wake began to lift our boat.

We wanted desperately for that to happen in clear visibility, even at the risk of being run down. If a ship was that near in broad daylight, we would probably find a way of making our presence known. But it did not happen, and daily our stocks fell; daily we grew weaker.

We would watch the vapour trails of jet aircraft flying at a great height, and we realised how tiny we were and how impossible it would be to see us. We marvelled at the thought that the distance we had taken weeks to cover could be flown in just a few hours. Once we saw two jets in the space of about four hours. The first was going towards Europe and the second was flying towards America. When Chay saw the second one he said, 'I wonder what that's going back for. Maybe it's Frank

Sinatra going back to New York. He must have forgotten his comics.'

We spent a great deal of our time looking at the sky, especially the night sky. There is something about it that brings you to yourself and makes you realise just how insignificant man is in the pattern of the universe. Often as I was rowing I would gaze up for minutes on end, spellbound by it all, but at the same time always feeling depressed afterwards. The cumulative effect of spending night after night in an open boat in the middle of the Atlantic, with the Plough, the North Star, Sirius and Mars always in the same position, gives you a feeling that you have made no progress at all during the day, that you are rowing your guts out and getting nowhere. If Chay was unable to sleep I would much sooner have a conversation with him. It helped pass the time and took us out of ourselves for a few minutes.

These conversations often started in the oddest of ways. I remember one night at this time when we were both so desperately worried about our position that we were turning more and more to each other for comfort, that we began talking about old age.

Chay suddenly said, 'You know, we are not the only ones on a short diet—what about the thousands of old-age pensioners who have nothing more to eat every day than us—you know a bit of old rice pudding for breakfast and a couple of biscuits and a beef cube for lunch; a cup of cocoa and a slice of bread before they go to bed. At least we're young and fit.'

That is the way we began to think. The night sky showed us we were a couple of scraps of nothing, and life seemed very short.

Soon I could hear him snoring under the canopy and I was alone with my own thoughts. As I rowed I gazed up at the sky. It was a wonderful night, with shooting stars crashing their way through the heavens. 'Dear God,' I murmured, 'please save us both.'

After two hours I called Chay to take his turn at the oars and I crawled into the shelter to try to sleep, but before doing so I wrote a few words in my log: '... Decide to eat this week's rations over fourteen days and then spread the last pack over twenty-eight days. This should achieve results.

'So impressive is the night that it is so hard not to believe there is some Almighty presence which orders these things. We both feel that we will finish all right and that, if we were to die, it would have happened already. We will walk off this boat humbler and more appreciative men, and possibly even a little wiser.

'At night there is much more time, when alone, to think of the more important things in life, such as family.'

Now we were down to half rations, with the prospect of quarter rations if we did not meet a ship. It was an interesting exercise in survival, and I felt that both of us would have plenty of useful things to tell the Army when we returned, but lack of food was having a very serious effect on our bodies. I had three boils, one on my left thigh which was most painful, and Chay was in just about the same condition.

I hoped that another month would see us at the end of our ordeal—although our reserves of strength were such that it was like reaching into the tin and finding there are no sweets left. The time factor, too, was becoming of increasing importance, because summer was just about at an end, and we would almost certainly perish in the equinoctial storms which were due a month later. Already the changing seasons were indicated by the flights of small birds we saw migrating south.

On Friday August 12 we washed and shaved, which made us feel better, but I noticed I had another two boils on my thighs, obviously due to the low calorie intake. I had a severe pain in my groin, indicating a serious poison build-up, and I pondered on the seemingly endless permutations of crises that can develop on such a venture. I wondered what problem we would be faced with next.

That night we nearly hit a huge baulk of floating teak covered with barnacles, and if there had been a collision in a storm then 'Rosie' might have sunk.

The incident was yet another piece in the rather morbid picture of our plight that we were building up in our minds. I remember Chay saying, 'It seems if they can't get us one way they'll get us another.'

We could see a lot of barnacles on 'Rosie's' side and on the rudder, some of them up to three inches long. We pulled off about half a dozen, leaving small parts of them still sticking to the boat. We realised it was futile to try to clear the sides alone and, because of the coldness of the water, we were not too keen to attempt to clear them from the boat's bottom.

The barnacles worried us. We knew we were collecting more of them every day, and we realised that they not only slowed us down, but made rowing far more strenuous. This was serious, as it used up precious energy. (We heard later that the *Queen Mary*, a somewhat bigger boat, was slowed-down considerably by the same complaint.)

The night passed as it usually did with both of us rowing two on two off, and we could not stop talking about the wonderful rainbow we had seen during the day. It was a magnificent sight. We could see both ends of it going straight into the water. Neither of us had much sleep. We just stayed awake talking and cheering each other up, and we continued rowing singly even after breakfast at about seven o'clock the following morning.

We decided alternate rowing was essential until we met a ship. It would have been too much of a drain on the little strength we had left for both of us to row.

Towards midday I was doing the rowing and Chay was sitting on a jerrycan in the stern and about to get us a bite to eat. Suddenly he gave a shout: 'A ship!'

I could hardly believe what he was saying. But he said it again. 'There it is—a ship!'

I thought I was dreaming. I dared to look round, and there it was, bow on to us, a tanker. Was I seeing things? My body began to tremble. My lips quivered. I thought I was going to cry. But there it was—a ship.

I saw Chay put his hands together. 'Thank God,' he said. 'Amen,' said I.

I leaped up from my seat, pulled out the wireless aerial and tied Chay's anorak to it. Chay got out our last flare and fired it. The ship saw it, and in a moment or two it was hard by us.

I have never seen anything so beautiful. That moment was all my Christmases and happy birthdays rolled into one. I was so happy, and Chay could not contain himself. He just laughed and laughed. I had never seen anybody so happy.

A man on the bridge shouted through a megaphone, 'Do you want anything? Are you all right?'

'We're okay,' I shouted, 'but we'd like some food.'

'How long for?' he shouted back.

'Two weeks,' yelled Chay.

I looked up to its great bulk towering above us and saw on the side of the ship the name *Haustellum*. We pulled closer to it and a ladder was lowered. The Captain appeared.

'Come aboard,' he said.

The boatswain, a Scotsman, came down the ladder. 'I'll look after your boat, lads. You go aboard.'

It was like a dream climbing the ladder to the steady deck of the tanker. We climbed with difficulty and, once on deck, we nearly fell over. It had been ten weeks since our legs had been used for walking.

The master, Captain Mitchell, a kindly man, shook hands with us and said, 'Now, gentlemen, what would you like to eat?'

Both of us knew exactly: scrambled eggs and huge 'doorsteps' of bread and butter and marmalade. And within a few minutes they came up by the plateful, straight from the galley to the captain's table. The clean linen tablecloth, the sparkling silver, the warmth, the smell of fresh-brewed coffee being poured into china—it was a memory that neither of us will ever forget.

Captain Mitchell asked us what fresh provisions we wanted. We told him: tins of food, fruit, milk, a torch and a knife. Everything was produced and packed in 'Rosie' for us, our photographs were taken by various members of the crew, and we must have shaken hands fifty times before we finally left.

It was an unforgettable meeting, and Chay and I climbed down the ladder full of gratitude. We settled down once again in 'Rosie' and pulled away with a strength that we had not felt for weeks. The crew of the *Haustellum* lined the decks to cheer us away, and we waved and waved until she was out of sight.

Now we felt we had no more worries. The food would quickly put new energy into us, and we pushed off on the last leg for home. Our hearts sang. Our prayers had been answered.

'Vous n'êtes pas loin'

Chay Blyth: August 14–22

'IT is uncanny how fortune has guided us across the ocean. It is almost as if some divine hand has created conditions to test and then guide us home.'

'I thanked the Lord for His help. I've been thinking of Maureen and Church. I'll step ashore a more humble, wiser and appreciative man.'

Our implicit faith in God, and our belief that it was largely due to His guidance that we had survived so far, is clearly evident in these excerpts taken from our daily log of August 14.

Neither of us considered our meeting with the *Haustellum* a lucky one. It was, we believed, a further proof that God was watching over us, and did not intend us to perish in His sea. As we took to the oars, surrounded by the life-saving rations, and with our backs still smarting from the farewell slaps of the *Haustellum*'s officers and crew, I closed my eyes and whispered a prayer of thanks.

It was a Sunday and our minds were filled with religious thoughts. What hypocrites we both were. It was expedient at the time to believe in God and have faith in His power to help us. We were up against it and wanted to rely on someone more powerful than ourselves to bring 'Rosie' safely home.

How strong was that faith? Well, for three weeks after we landed I didn't set foot in a church. Neither did John. Our rock-like belief began to crumble the moment our feet were back on solid ground. We feel much closer to God now than we did before setting out on our journey, but it is a pale shadow of the religious fervour that gripped us in mid-Atlantic.

I think it true that most people find it convenient to call on God in moments of danger. The fellow in a plane which develops engine trouble says, 'O God. Please help me.' Half an hour later after it lands safely he rushes straight for the bar. He doesn't think of going to a church and offering a prayer of thanks for his safe delivery.

And so it was with us.

The cheerful blast of the *Haustellum*'s whistle, sounding the 'Bon Voyage' signal, echoed in our minds for hours after she slipped out of sight below the Western horizon. We had supplies to keep us going on full rations for a further month—they had loaded the boat for us, and we spent the next two hours sorting all the stores out. We were surprised at the amount they had given us—water too, and Captain Mitchell contributed a box of his own biscuits.

Haustellum also gave us a full confirmation of our position and enough new information to provide topics for discussion and speculation for a week.

We were thrilled but surprised to learn that England had won the World Cup. Ramsay's Rovers had come in for so much criticism during the weeks prior to our leaving London that we had not expected them to get beyond the first round.

'I wish it had happened abroad though,' said John. 'You can bet your life the foreigners are all saying it was a pre-arranged result.'

He sat astride a jerrycan in the stern, clutching an empty milk carton 'microphone' at his chin, and gave a heavily accented commentary on the final as seen by a German, a Frenchman and a South American. I took the part of crowd, referee and players. The 'game' broke up in gales of laughter when I attempted a penalty kick from the forward seat and landed on my backside squarely on a tin of corned beef.

John was in considerable pain when it came to his turn to row. He had strained his left shoulder holding the mooring rope thrown down by the *Haustellum* and was unable to pull strongly with that arm. So that we should not keep circling to the left he was forced to reduce pressure on the right oar too, and for almost a day our speed was cut down while John was at the oars.

We had both, predictably enough, eaten considerably too much of the rich food offered us in the *Haustellum* Captain's cabin. Thickly spread butter with mounds of marmalade. Just thinking of it brought a rush of saliva to my salt-dried mouth.

But poor John had no such happy memories. By midnight his forehead and cheeks glistened with sweat and his face had turned quite pale under its tan. Every few moments he clutched at his stomach and groaned. As I watched him suffer from my position at the oars a dozen unpleasant images flashed through my head. John in high fever from a virus picked up from the crew. Food poisoning. Sun stroke. Having been out of contact with every kind of land infection for so long, I feared that our blood had become weakened and was not up to fighting off the sickness bugs.

In his log John recorded, briefly: 'As we went into the night I decided to unload my system of some of the excess food which I had eaten. Once I had made myself sick my general condition improved. We have overestimated the immediate effect of more food and find the night-time most tiring.'

I fared slightly better, but I, too, found that the increased amount of food we were able to eat, far from giving extra energy, made me want to sleep all the time.

It was a scorching hot day. A heat haze hung low on the water, and to touch the boat's paintwork with our bare skin meant a sharp pain. My hands were very sore with double heads forming on the callouses on my palms. Several times I dozed off while rowing, and only the jerk on my arms as the waves snatched at the oars kept me from spending the whole of my two-hour 'stag' asleep.

We tried rowing together—but had to give it up. We found that after a couple of hours we were both absolutely fagged out and we had to sleep for an hour. This meant no progress.

It took more than three days, with regular doses of vitamin pills, to get back to normal, and during that time we lived in a dream-like state midway between waking and sleeping. Nothing we did seemed to be really happening. It was just as though we were sitting outside the boat watching two other blokes doing the work for us. Even the sea seemed dull and tired, and our conversations ended in midstream.

A member of the *Haustellum*'s crew had told us that according to newspaper reports when they left England, Johnstone and Hoare were only five hundred miles out. We automatically assumed they meant five hundred miles out of Land's End, which by this time would place them four to five hundred miles ahead of us. We were happy that they should get in first, but we wanted to complete the crossing in a shorter time.

Now it looked as though they were going to beat us on both counts. I was happy for them that they should be home in another week, but in my mind they were still our rivals, and I hated the thought of being beaten.

Our discussion on this was typical of the half-finished conversations I associate with this trance-like period.

John was rowing and I was sitting cross-legged in the stern opening a tin of Spam.

'I suppose that's it, then,' I said.

'What?' He gave the word an extra syllable.

'A week. They'll be in in a week.'

'Who?'

'The *Puffin*. Who do you think?'

I had levered the cold meat out of the tin before he answered.

'What makes you say that?'

'Well, you said it yourself, yesterday.'

'Did I?'

'Yes.'

I broke the Spam into two portions and reached for the dry biscuits.

'If they were five hundred miles out a week ago they've only a week to go. We're still over seven hundred from England.'

I ate my lunch and changed places with him at the oars.

'We can still chop a few days off their time if we hurry,' he said in between mouthfuls of Spam.

I bent my head and pulled harder.

'How much longer?' It did not seem at all strange that he did not answer. A good five minutes later I looked up and saw that John was asleep.

Suddenly there was a tremendous crash. The boat stopped dead and I tumbled backwards off the seat, sending the oar blades groping for the sky. John was on his feet in a second, the sleep and tiredness shocked out of him. He staggered as something heavy shuddered along the side and set the boat rocking.

'For God's sake what happened?' he bellowed.

'We hit something. Don't know what it was, but it might have cracked the hull.'

I thrust the oars into place along the sides and started digging the ration packs and water containers from their place at the bow just to check for a leak.

'I can see it now,' said John calmly. 'It's a big teak log. We must have run into it head on.'

I looked over the side. The log was about twelve feet long and very thick. If we had been in a heavy sea and had met the force of the log moving towards us it would certainly have caused very severe damage.

There was always a certain amount of water slopping about the floorboards, and it was difficult to tell straight away if we had sprung a leak. I finished moving the equipment from the bow, and getting down on our hands and knees we made an inch by inch inspection of the hull.

'No damage here,' said John. He leaned over the side and probed the underwater sections of the bow with his fingers. 'There's a mark along the side just below the waterline, but the hull hasn't split,' he reported.

John helped me replace the tins and packages in their place and went back to the sleeping position. 'Do you feel like carrying on?' he asked.

I nodded. 'Do we keep on the same course?'

'Yes. 045 degrees.'

It was a soul-destroying course. It meant that every mile we covered actually took us only a half mile nearer England. But it was necessary if we were to avoid landing in France or heading up the English Channel.

I thought of Johnstone and Hoare in *Puffin*. We had not been given an exact position for them, and I wondered if they were in a similar spot to ourselves—either north or south of their required course and wasting valuable energy without getting appreciably nearer to home.

My thoughts flitted from Johnstone to home, and from home to Scotland. I thought about my friends in the sergeant's mess at Aldershot, of what my first child would look like—I thought about anything to keep my mind occupied and stop me falling asleep. Anything that is except the callouses on my hands and the foul taste of the drinking water and soggy, salt-invaded biscuits.

These were the moments of my personal battle against the sea—the long, tedious hours when I rowed and John slept. You never know how brave you are or how tough you are until your life depends on your courage, and after seventy-three days at sea my own courage was beginning to ebb away.

Those lonely hours dragged past as though each moment was slowly dripping the length of the oars. In mounting storm or in the awed, almost cathedral-like quiet of a dead calm my mind would become prey to all kinds of fanciful fears, and underlying everything was the growing conviction that we were fated to be out there for ever. Was the strain proving too much for us? Were we reaching breaking-point?

The small white terns, which we had several times watched in aerial combat, were to teach us a valuable lesson. A big gull was keeping us company, flying beside 'Rosie', soaring up and down, only a foot from the undulating waves, with wonderful control. Then the terns appeared. One by one they swooped at the gull, who was at least five times their size, until one little chap, his legs held stiffly in front of him, dive-bombed the gull's back, pushing him, with a thwack, into the sea.

The gull flew off, defeated.

That was the great thing, to win. The completion of each two-hour 'stag' was a little victory. Monotony, physical tiredness and 'mental plonk' were the losers.

One evening as I dreamt, argued and cursed my way through another solitary spell on the oars I witnessed one of those incredibly beautiful occurrences the sea threw our way from time to time. I suddenly found myself rowing through acres of fish. The sight astonished me. I could not begin to believe what I was seeing.

There seemed to be millions of them. It was already growing dark, and each fish left a long phosphorescent trail as it moved. As far as I could see in all directions the sea was alive with seething, fast-moving lights.

I stopped rowing and woke John. It was the only big shoal of fish we had seen on the whole trip, and I did not want him to miss it. The fish were six to nine inches long, silver, with a spike on the nose. It must have taken about ten minutes for them to pass by.

'That's the sort of shoal a fisherman dreams of finding,' said John. 'You could fill a whole boat in half a day.'

By this time we were both responding to the improved diet, though eating too much to make precious use of the fresh food before it went bad.

Sane conversation became possible again, and John resumed his French tuition. I was now able to count up to a hundred in French and manage a number of simple questions and answers. Perhaps because of my Scottish accent, or it may have been the 'mental plonk', I found great difficulty in remembering 'une', 'vingt et un' and 'onze'.

But John was equally slow in picking up some of the moves in chess. I had started giving him lessons about the third week out and was annoyed that we had not brought a miniature chess board with us.

Sitting down to play chess had not been one of our plans when we prepared for the crossing. We had, with short-sighted optimism, assumed we could row every day, and that there would not be time for playing games. How wrong we were. There were days when I would have given everything I owned in exchange for a chess board or a child's ludo set.

It was not until August 17 that we decided to 'go fishing'. Up to then we had not seriously attempted to fish at all. We had thrown a line to trail overboard once or twice when we saw fish, with no success. Now, for the first time, the opportunity arose to try a little sport.

John is a fanatical fisherman. It is an obsession with him. He spent hours explaining the snags and intricacies of salmon and trout fishing, the differences between fresh and sea-water angling and the history of a dozen different species. I had done a little river fishing in Scotland. Now I was being introduced to sea angling. I even knew that sharks had been knocking about for more than two hundred thousand years. John had even resigned his commission at one stage to start a shark-fishing business in Scotland. But that venture failed.

On the morning of August 17 we were bemoaning the fact that our helpful south-west wind was veering round to the East when John caught sight of a large fish, just below the surface, a few feet away from the boat.

'Chay, let's try catching the devil,' he said.

He dropped the cooking pot he had been cleaning and scrabbled about in his pile of equipment, surfacing a few seconds later and triumphantly displaying two lines and a box of hooks.

'Now, what shall we use as bait?'

After another brief search he produced a jar of pork rind which he had bought in America.

Our first attempts to catch the fish were a complete failure. John handed me a treble hook and a lump of bread.

'You have a go with this,' he said.

I leaned over the stern and dangled the bait a few feet in front of the fish's nose. It flicked its tail and closed the gap to about an inch. I glanced at John, and he was grinning.

'Come on you idiot, bite.'

The fish nosed forward and opened its mouth. I was trembling with excitement. Just a few more seconds, then:

'Got him.'

I gripped the line and started to haul in. But it wasn't going to be that easy. The fish struggled and I pulled. Suddenly the line came free. The hook had come loose. In a flash the fish had gone, tail flapping madly.

'Blast!'

John patted my shoulder. 'Don't worry. You'll probably get the next one. But make sure the hook is firmly lodged before you start pulling it in.'

He produced a thing shaped like a miniature shoe-horn which had a fierce-looking hook dangling underneath.

'This is a four-inch silver ripper spoon,' he announced authoritatively. 'This should do the trick.'

With practised fingers he slipped a piece of pork rind on to the hook and cast it over the side. Twenty seconds later there was a jerk on the line and a mad threshing in the water. John hauled in the line with a firm, easy action, and suddenly our first catch was flapping about in the bottom of the boat.

We both grinned from ear to ear, changed places and John gave me the ripper spoon to try. In three minutes we had caught three more of the same species. They were bluish grey in colour, with silver flanks and a white belly and weighed between four and five pounds. The dorsal fin was in two parts, the first with spines. John thought they were bass, considered by many fishermen to be one of the best sea-angling fishes.

'I think they flourish off the coast of Spain and Portugal,' he said. 'But you may get them in northern waters, in the Channel and off the southern coasts of Britain.'

He told me they fed on small fishes like sea-eels, sprat and pilchards.

'They've also got a hell of a stink,' I said and held a handkerchief to my nose.

The fish were still flapping about the bottom boards, and after taking pictures of them, we managed, after a tussle, to get them over the side. However, they avenged their defeat on John. The tiny, needle-sharp spines pricked one of his fingers and it was painful for days afterwards. It was a small injury, but it had to be watched closely for signs of infection.

By late that evening we were making no headway at all in the face of a strong east wind and put out the sea anchor. We hoped the changeable weather would see the east wind out during the night. So cursing the wind, the sea and the inevitable rain, we crawled under the canvas for another miserable night, having made less than five miles in the direction of home.

The grim, unending battle against the wind and rain continued all the next day. Rowing together we were able to make a little headway and the miles rolled tortuously under our boat.

At three o'clock we stopped for a blow and I retreated under the canopy to make cocoa. There was little use in being under cover from the point of view of personal comfort. We were both soaked to the skin, and no amount of rain and spray could make us any wetter.

John sat in the open, shielding his eyes from the spray and pulling the boat into the wind. I shouted that the cocoa was ready and he looked up.

Then he scrambled towards me. 'There's a boat out there,' he yelled, pointing into the wind.

I looked round the cover and saw a light blue fishing boat only a few hundred yards from us. She was making straight towards us and must have seen our boat several minutes before John spotted her. It was a French tuna boat with great, line-trailing outriggings on either side.

Three crew men lined the rail. We could see their mouths working, but the words were carried away by the wind. The boat had the word *Etel* painted on the stern, but that's all we learned about her. She passed us at a distance of one hundred yards, and though we screamed for a position through cupped hands, the fishermen just shook their heads. They couldn't hear us.

An hour later we saw a second tuna boat and a tanker heading East. But they were too far away to signal.

Then in the deepening gloom we saw a third tuna boat—the *Paul et Virginie*. She had her lines hauled in and came within twenty yards of us.

I took the chart from its cover and opened it out. John shouted for a position in French, and I pointed to the chart. Finally, the skipper understood and disappeared into the wheel-house, probably to consult his own chart. He came out carrying a megaphone.

'Quarante-huit et dix-neuf,' he roared. 'Avez-vous besoin de quelque chose?'

John shook his head.

'Comment vous appelez-vous?'

'Ridgway et Blyth,' I shouted. 'Et *English Rose trois*.'

It was the first time I had spoken French to anyone, but John and the skipper seemed to understand.

'Bravo,' he replied. 'Vous n'êtes pas loin.'

The crew made an exaggerated pretence of rowing. 'Encore, encore,' they yelled and gave the thumbs up sign.

'What's pas loin mean?' I asked John.

'Not far,' he said. 'Not far with an engine, but still a damned long way for us.'

We watched the *Paul et Virginie* until she was out of sight. The ever-rising wind had whipped the waves to a height of ten feet, and she was being badly thrown about.

'I don't fancy being in that in this weather,' I told John.

He gave me one incredulous look and burst out laughing.

'What's so funny?'

'You. You'd hate to be in that tuna boat in this weather. What do you think it's like in this one—a joy-ride?'

I had become so used to the movement of 'Rosie' that I had forgotten for a moment where I was. But the French boat was plunging and rolling so badly I had been quite sorry for the men on board. In fact, we were being thrown about worse than they were. I hadn't really thought how we must have looked to them.

All that night and the next day we were forced to ride our sea anchor. Our clothes and the spare blankets were disintegrating rapidly and scarcely blocked the wind and cold at all. Confined to our sleeping places, together by this time to give mutual protection from the cold, we almost wept with frustration.

A brief try at rowing on August 19 was worse than useless. With the sea anchor taken in we were losing more distance than we could possibly make up rowing.

And on top of everything else John's rash was spreading down from his neck, and I was beginning to itch all over. The salt, having soaked through all our layers of clothing, was certainly getting to work on our skin. The itching was driving us crazy. The pain in my knees, after two days and nights of being bent double, was excruciating. To straighten them was worse. The first few inches were moments of searing agony. The rest of the way was sudden bliss as the pain seeped away.

August 20 came and went. A fearful night of rain and sleeplessness gave way to a day of the most settled east winds since that dreadful week at 40 degrees West. I thought of the millions of British holidaymakers relaxing on beaches around the country, and gloomily watched the dory slipping west on the sea anchor. Fifty million Britons hoping it will last, while we two pray for the wild, wet westerly that spells home for us and ruined holidays for those at the seaside.

On August 21 we managed, by rowing together, to make a little headway. But strangely enough my main concern was the length of my hair. I longed for a haircut and a shampoo, and would have paid a fiver for the pleasure of it.

I have seldom been so deeply unhappy for so many short periods for such a long time. I tried to keep in mind Mrs. Moore's words: 'Above all you will need patience.' How right she was. Eighty days in an open boat and we were coming apart at the seams.

Even a wash and a shave the following day failed to raise our morale. Grey heavy seas matched our grey mood. We were reaching breaking-point fast now—and both knew it.

Terns, fulmars and black-headed gulls switching back and forth over the boat fixed our thoughts firmly on land. Would we ever see it again? If the east wind had its way we never would. That night found us rowing desperately to the North-east on the brink of absolute despair.

Despair

John Ridgway: August 23–31

It was now getting more and more awful as we travelled further and further towards the north. Summer seemed to be over, the nights were getting longer and colder. As each hour succeeded monotonous hour we were getting progressively weaker, both mentally and physically. Everything was becoming more and more of an effort.

We rowed together the whole of that Tuesday, August 23, in a gathering southerly to south-westerly wind. We saw nothing all day on the grey, heavy seas, except the occasional fishing buoy or cork. It was really astonishing to find so much rubbish in the middle of an ocean. Those bits of cork we saw must have been washed all the way across the Atlantic. They might even belong to some of our friends in the fishing fleet back in Orleans.

We had missed two or three days writing up our logs and spent part of the day catching up. I found that the days seemed to merge one into the other now. Last Sunday seemed a long way away and I had to strain my mind to try to remember what had happened. You lose any sense of time and the happenings get out of place. I could not remember, for instance, if one incident on the Sunday had happened before supper or after. That was only forty-eight hours earlier. I had to check with Chay to get things right. It was just another pointer towards our mental deterioration.

The waters were really deserted in that spot on the

ocean. A gannet appeared and the usual collection of Mother Cary's chickens, black caps, browns, terns and fulmars. I tried to pass some of the time to try to take my mind off our desperate state by watching the birds wheel and bank. It was all so easy and effortless. I began to wish I could grow wings and take off into the dusk for Ireland. I do not know how fast these big birds fly. But it would only be a couple of days before they could get the scent of a peat fire or catch the glint of light in some lonely cottage window. How I envied their ability to choose land when they wished. We just had to flog along as best we could. There was no choice for us. It was hard labour all the way.

Late that night the wind went firmly round to the South, and once again we began to be blown north. We rowed on desperately, wondering if the west winds had abandoned us and the Atlantic for ever.

Just after midnight Chay and I called it a day and got down together in the bottom of the boat. We dozed fretfully as the storm rose and 'Rosie' began again that crazy, bucketing motion that wears one down so.

At one o'clock, at a time when our spirits were at their lowest, we were hit by a huge wave. It curled over the side of the boat and we were half filled with this ice-cold water before we realised what had happened. We fought our way out of the tarpaulin that seemed to have wrapped itself around us like a winding sheet. It was pitch black; we could see nothing.

By instinct we found our buckets and bailed and bailed. The wind had got up to storm strength so suddenly that it nearly overwhelmed us. We bailed all night. And when we did not bail we pumped at that everlasting steady, dreary pace—pump, pump and pump, pump.

If only I could express the misery of it all. For seven hours, and nearly every one of them as black as the in-

side of a coal bunker, we hung on to life grimly. We
were wet through. Chay's rubber suit was frayed right
through and water soaked on to his bottom and his
back and around tears in the arms. My suit was torn
across the chest, and water just poured on to my stomach
—cold water. I had never felt so cold in the whole of my
life despite the hard work that I did through the night
hours.

I wondered why we went on. Why did we not just sit
down and call it a day. Death would be peace, all peace,
from this agony. We went on though, for, as Chay is
always saying, we have a taste for pain. I wondered how
true this was and whether we were not sick, social mis-
fits.

I wondered that I had time to philosophise in the
middle of that awful night which was just a haze of
waves and water howling at us and being cut to pieces
by the flying spray and spume. It must have been some
sort of defence mechanism which twisted my mind away
from our present dangers to an inner consideration of
the reason why.

When I was not numbed of thought and action I
prayed. I remembered that ancient prayer which took
on such a new meaning, the prayer for those in peril on
the seas. I would never again gabble through set prayers
as I had in the past. Then they were just a routine set of
sentences that really did not strike home. But in the
future when they prayed for those in peril on the sea my
heart would go out to those seamen the world over who
were in storm or tempest or hurricane or just plain
terror. There would be meaning then—I would pray as
someone who knew the sea for all my brothers on the
deep waters.

How I wished that we had a cabin to climb into and
get away from the eternal wetness and cold. As I continued to bail with Chay I imagined how good it would

be to have a decent fug up and be able to keep warm. We were getting far to the north, and had no refuge to look forward to. I became more and more frightened, not that we were going to be killed instantly but by the slow wearing-down process of the storm and its attendant cold and wet. Exposure was a definite risk, and if we suffered from exposure there was no hospital bed and hot bottles and a pretty nurse to make us better again.

We drifted all that long night; we were not concerned where we were going. Survival was all we cared about. At about 8 a.m. we stopped pumping as the seas went down just a little and the wind dropped from storm to gale. We had come through again, but we were mighty close to the end of our tether now. Physical and mental weariness possessed us both. The end of the journey could not come quickly enough.

We crawled together under the tarpaulin. We were wet and cold, but at least we were out of the direct blast of the winds and the water only dripped on us here instead of falling on us like a bath being emptied.

We stayed there, not talking, hardly dozing, until 1 p.m. when we crawled out like drowned rats. I made an automatic check of our equipment, rather like an airline pilot who is able to see all his instruments at one quick glance. The glance would tell him if anything was out of the ordinary. My glance showed me that all was well with 'Rosie'. She was a splendid boat.

I took the oars for half an hour while Chay made some curry and cocoa. He really did do well on the cooking side. He never once ruined a meal, or upset our pressure cooker, irrespective of the state of the seas or however hard 'Rosie' rolled. We sipped gently at that hot cocoa. It brought us back to life. It was one of the greatest drinks I had ever had.

We shared the curry in the same old way. Chay used

the wooden spoon first and then handed me the still steaming curry and rice in the pan.

He had hardly eaten any.

'You're generous all of a sudden, Chay.'

'No, not generous—I just don't want any more, that's all.'

I took the spoon and took two or three mouthfuls. It was a great big helping I had got, and yet the stuff seemed to be sticking in my throat like hot glue. I remembered the times I had envied every mouthful that Chay ate, the times when I could have eaten half a dozen curries on my own.

I pushed the pan away. 'Finish it, Chay.'

'Really, I couldn't take another mouthful.'

'No, I can't either. What shall we do with it, throw it away?'

'Yes,' Chay replied. 'It won't keep.'

So we ladled it into the water, and we were very glad to see the mush disappear. Some of our seagull friends swooped on the unexpected feast, and we had a battle royal around 'Rosie' as the birds fought and wrestled for our rice and bits of meat.

'What's wrong with us, Chay?' I asked. 'You're the expert on grub and calories.'

'I don't know. I think we've just over-exerted ourselves and this is our bodies telling us to knock off and take it easy for a bit.'

But we could not afford to take it easy. It was painful to have to go on, but we had to. So we rowed all day, still wet and with a big swell running.

I took a brief break to set the Sarbe going again as it was a Thursday. But there was still no sign of the Royal Air Force. I just could not understand this, as the set was waterproofed and I knew it had been working properly before we sailed. We put down the non-arrival of the

R.A.F. to the fact that we were abandoned and no one really cared where we were.

So we rowed on and on. I rowed the first night 'stag' that evening from 9 to 11 p.m., and it seemed as though an unseen hand was pulling us back towards America. I just could not get the boat to move through the water. Chay and I were now getting desperate, and this failure to get the boat moving depressed me even more. I believed that my muscles were seizing up and that all my energy was expended. Or was it those barnacles?

I woke Chay at eleven and told him that the wind which earlier had been a Storm Force 10 from the South, had gone round to the East and was building up.

'Chay, we just cannot go on like this pulling against an easterly wind. We'll just have to accept that we'll lose ground. We must have some reserve of strength left. We were nearly finished by that storm. We are all that much weaker now. Don't forget, if we give the sea an inch it will have us.'

Chay looked at me and, I suppose, saw me as I really was—despondent, wet, harassed, cold and frightened. He was not quite as bad as me, as he had had two hours off under the canvas.

'You're right, John. We'll put the sea anchor out and try and get some sleep. It's the only sensible thing to do.'

I went to stream the sea anchor. As I let it slide over the side I found my hands rubbing against a rope in the darkness. I pulled at it. It came in very slowly. The coil of rope for the sea anchor had come undone unknown to us, and a loop of it had been trailing under the boat.

I felt a bit better immediately. This was the 'unseen hand' that had pulled me back during the 'stag'. 'Rosie' rode to the anchor as the first blasts of an easterly gale lifted her bows.

And so we lay for the rest of the night filled with misery and cold, the seas roaring by our resting-place only a few inches away and all the time the noise of the wind. It was like being on a railway station with expresses passing through every half minute—that was the noise that persisted all night through as we cowered under the tarpaulin.

The night passed somehow. It seemed to last a year, but it came to the end eventually. I pushed back the tarpaulin and made my automatic glance around the boat. She was still all right, the gear was still all there. I looked towards the East and then South-east and massive seas were rolling in. I crawled back under the tarpaulin cover and the blanket.

'There's no point in trying anything in this, Chay. We'll just have to sweat a bit more and hope that the bloody wind will finally go round to the West and die down a bit,' I said. And Chay agreed after casting one eye over the gunwale and seeing the state of the Atlantic.

We spent the next two hours yarning. We were always talking on any subject that came into our heads. That morning it was films—especially Westerns. We went through all the plots of every Western we had ever seen. Our favourite was *High Noon*. We had a sort of Gallup Poll on which was the finest we had seen and gave ratings from 'excellent' to 'poor'. John Huston's films we rated 'excellent'.

I did not know that then, but within the fortnight I was to meet John Huston. It happened three days after we arrived in Ireland. Chay and I and our wives were sitting together at the back of a B.E.A. Viscount coming from Shannon to London when I heard the hostess say: 'Certainly, Mr. Huston.' I looked across the gangway and saw the weather-beaten face of a man sitting on his own on the rear seat.

I went over and asked him if he were THE Mr. Huston. He was, and he invited me to sit with him. I spent the rest of the trip to London on that fine, sunny lunchtime, talking to this man about the plots of his films which had helped us through our worst morning ever at sea.

For that day, after two hours of film talk, I saw our emergency radio tucked away in the corner of 'Rosie'. Chay and I are professional soldiers in the Parachute Regiment. Our whole lives had been moulded to succeed. If we are told to run ten miles, we run them. If we are told to climb a mountain, we climb it. Chay and I have always succeeded in the past and overcome any hazard that the Army has put in our way. We approached the Atlantic in the same way. It was a challenge, and once we had decided to start our whole training insisted that we finish.

August 26 was a bad day for us. The sea would not give us a chance to dry our clothes, and thinking about the dangerous cliffs along the Irish coast made me anxious about our landfall. The coast and the proximity of equinoctial gales added up to a very difficult landing operation. We could board the next ship met—we were very near the North American shipping lane again. Should we give up? Our logs described our reactions. Chay wrote:

'We stayed in bed most of the day. I tried to get dried-out, but it proved to be unsuccessful. All I am anxious to get done was get my socks a splashing.

'We are pretty low morale-wise. We discussed the event of pulling the Red Handle and calling it a day.'

The Red Handle was a trip mechanism on our Sarbe set. A piece of string, with a red-painted toggle on the end of it, was attached to a pin on the set. A tug on the toggle pulled out the pin and automatically released a small aerial, and the set immediately began transmitting an emergency signal, which could be picked up by aircraft.

Chay's log continued: 'It has got to be thought of, but I believe this will never happen. I can't see either of us giving up.

'We just lay under the blankets and talked about pictures we had seen, telling each other of the plot.

'One of the blankets has a great tear in it. I think it was done by me. These blankets are our very lives.

'The canopy hollows in the middle and the rain continually drips through. We have two sticks to hold it up. It helps, but not all that much. It's really pretty grim underneath, and now we are shivering with cold.'

That same day I wrote:

'All day massive seas rolled up from S.E.

'We tried to sleep and talked over all the plots of all the Western films we had ever seen.

'At 09.30 I gave Blyth the opportunity to call it a day if he wished. I pointed out the hazards of a landfall on the cliffs of the South-west coast of Eire. He is enormously strong and said "Go on" without hesitation. If he wants to go on, then I shall go on—why, I can't tell you, but I must and I will just go on and on and on.

'A desperate night of wet and cold; luckily the seas did not break into "Rosie" very often.

'I now have another boil on my backside, and Blyth has a very sore backside, and is itching all over. Still, I think he sings like a thrush! He also has salt-water sores all over his hands.

'If we meet a ship we shall give the impression of great fitness. Why, why, why?'

So the decision was made.

'Well,' I said, 'if we've decided to row the Atlantic— we'll bloody well row it.'

We will get through now, I thought, as the pair of us set to again.

We were still wet and cold. But there seemed to be a new sense of purpose about 'Rosie' and her crew. As if Chay sensed this, he burst into song, and this time he outdid everything he had ever done before. The songs fairly rolled out. Scots ballads, marching songs, even 'Strangers in the Night', although, to be fair, he could not quite give the Frankie touch to that one.

It bucked us up quite a bit. In fact, I thought we both looked extremely fit. When we are next sighted, I thought, they will not believe what we have been through and how low we are in spirits and in physical fitness. We shall. We know that we shall live in a daze for weeks after we get back to land. But that is the important point—we shall know what we have been through, even if other people are disbelieving.

We woke early the next morning, Saturday, August 27. As we started rowing I wondered if Marie-Christine was awake yet and whether she was at our own home or still with her relatives in Ireland. She must be getting anxious.

The sun came out early and the wind switched round suddenly to the South-west, a nice pleasant zephyr of a wind. I just thought what fools we would have looked if someone had come to pick us up this morning. We would have felt very ashamed.

As the sun got hotter we took our clothes off and hung them up to dry. We both washed and shaved, and Chay even managed to get his mop of black hair shampooed. He looked like a Teddy Boy with that mop, not like a Parachute Sergeant.

While he was rowing steadily at 2.30 p.m. Chay suddenly shouted, 'Get dressed, quickly.' I was shaving.

I thought he had had a sudden attack of modesty. But he added a moment or so later, 'Yes, she's coming our way. It's a ship.'

I scrambled into some trousers, and so did Chay. The bath and shave and the sun had partly overcome an earlier depression when I found that a sight put us only

187

at 19 degrees West. All my depression was lifted now as I saw the ship stop not far away and we rowed alongside her.

The ship was a Finn, the *Finnalpino*. As we shouted up at them we realised that their English was poor. They beckoned us up. I went aboard while Chay held 'Rosie' a few feet off the ship's side. He said later that he had a chat with some of the passengers as 'Rosie' was lifted up seven feet and down seven feet by the slight swell. He was a bit worried that he would let 'Rosie' hit the side.

The Finns were very kind to us. I got a position from her Captain which put us at 52 degrees 17 minutes North, 17 degrees 42 minutes West. In other words, my own position was one degree out. I suppose that is what comes of trying to take an accurate sight in a rocking small boat—one just cannot be accurate all the time. This meant that we were only two hundred and fifty miles from Ireland—a week from home!

They told us that they would report us to Lloyd's and say that we were making for Valentia Island, Eire. They also gave us stores, fresh fruit, bread, jam and so on.

The Captain, who spoke quite adequate English, said that he had seen us on television in Europe. He also said that Johnstone in the *Puffin* was still out in the middle somewhere. I hoped to God that was not right.

When I got down to 'Rosie' again we were laden with goodies that the ship had given us. We were all right for food now, and had only a little distance to go.

Although the Captain's English was good, it was not as good as I thought. He could not have understood my statement that we were headed for Valentia. This led to some sadness on our part when we arrived. We found that instead of our wives waiting for us in Ireland, they had waited in the Scilly Isles, and this meant that they were not on the quayside to greet us when we hit Ireland.

Our decision to make for Ireland had been made before we sighted the *Finnalpino*. I decided that the nearest land was our objective. I did not trust the English weather in September. It would have been stupid to have turned right and headed for Land's End and got drowned in the Channel. Ireland for us then. But even that was up to the weather. It only had to go round to the North-west again and we would have ended up in Land's End whether we wanted to or not.

Later that evening we saw two huge birds, almost prehistoric they looked. They had a golden-coloured head, mainly white on top but with black speckles underneath. They each had a very long and pointed beak. I had no idea what they were. They were about the size of swans, I suppose, with very long white bodies. I think they were gannets.

We were rowing very hard again now, and 'Rosie' seemed to realise that land was near, for she seemed to shoot over the water. I shall never, never regret having picked her. I cannot think of any finer boat for this sort of venture.

We had no radio now, of course. That was another thing that the sea managed to kill. But we were both glad, surprisingly. Since it went our sense of comradeship had grown much stronger. We had to make our own amusements, such as Chay singing or our yarns through the days, talking of old times and of our experiences in the service. Films and Frank Sinatra were two topics that we never seemed to tire of. We would certainly like to meet this man Frankie.

We had a feast that evening as the sun was setting. It was a glorious end to what had been a very fortunate day for us, so we meant to celebrate it. We picked on for our feast—of all things—jam butties. We ate them until we looked like them. And then some oranges and apples.

Real fresh fruit full of vitamin C. But it was not the vitamins, it was the taste we were interested in.

We had a good night and woke up to more jam butties for breakfast on August 29, as well as some more fruit. This is the trouble with really fresh food—it goes off very quickly. Bread soon becomes uneatable, as the sea air gets at it, and fruit rots in a day or two. As for the eggs we managed to get, these got broken in the first heavy seas. That is why it was so important to have good dehydrated foods packed tightly in plastic packs. Even some of those were ruined.

Looking back, it was not a very good night, as the wind freshened and blew Force 5 for most of it, and then blustered up to a full gale Force 8 by dawn. It just goes to show that with a full belly one's difficulties are lessened. Bless those Finns and their kindness.

Chay and I discussed what we would need to do when we landed and before we landed. That position of only two hundred and fifty miles to go really got us talking about nothing except land and landings.

We decided that once we sighted land, which would probably be from about eight miles if it is a high cliff, we would stream the sea anchor while we prepared a plan. We did not want to land in the dark.

We decided that our films, written logs, letters to our wives and cameras must be in a light, waterproof container which would be tied to one of us so that they would not get washed away. It would be dreadful to have come all that way and not have a thing to show for it.

We decided that we must also have at hand ropes, storm rations and rockets, just in case we should be thrown on to rocks and have to swim for it. We must think ahead to spending a day or so in an isolated part of West Ireland miles from any house. It would be a bit stupid to be found dead of starvation on land!

If we did swim for it and make it all right we thought we might fire our rockets. The main reason would be to try to alert a coastguard. But partly as a celebration. I think a salvo of red and white rockets with half a dozen day green smoke signals on the coast would be a fair way to express our relief.

The routine if we landed at a beach would, of course, be very different. We would not have our Brock's Benefit night, but we would pull 'Rosie' well clear of the water and remain with her until someone arrived. This is mainly because of our affection for this marvellous boat, but partly to see that no children found our medicine chest with its gaily coloured pills, which could probably be very dangerous if they were chewed up.

We also realised that if we had been in newspapers and on television in many parts of the world as the Finns had told us, then there might be souvenir hunters about. In fact, these gentlemen were to cause us some trouble after we landed. We had had our gear stowed by the magnificent lifeboatmen of the Aran Isles in their lifeboat house at Inishmore for twenty-four hours after we landed there. They, being great seamen, knew the value of our stores and were interested by our track charts, which we showed them, and the six-inch sextant that had brought us to a safe landing.

All these things were safely returned to us when we left for the mainland and then on to London. But when 'Rosie' and the gear reached London we found the sextant, half the track chart, all the rowlocks except one pair and various other small pieces of gear had disappeared. I know I could have wept when Chay came back from the storeroom to tell me of our losses. These things were old friends who had served us well. I do not like souvenir hunters.

That was all in the future, but our preparations for

landing did at least show that we still retained a certain amount of forethought. That was the result of our increased morale and the fresh food, I was sure.

Having made our plans for landing, we came back to the present again and found it was not pleasant. Chay had salt-water sores at each wrist where his suit rubbed against his wrist at each stroke of the oar, and there was an ugly rash on his feet which made them both painful and itching.

Both of us had very stiff and painful knee joints. It is not natural for a man to sit down for three months and not walk around in a normal way. I suppose this is why prisoners in jails are given an hour's walk round and round the jailyard each morning. We had been prisoners in an eight by four cage without bars for three months without the benefit of a morning jaunt. We both prayed that there would be no permanent harm from this trip. I was rather worried about Chay's hands. He still could not clench them, and they looked cracked and calloused.

We rowed during that day on a general heading of East, taking it in turns to pump as the north-westerly gale buried 'Rosie's' nose in the swells off and on and brought gallons of water in. Those pumps had been marvellous. They gave us no trouble at all. They saved our lives time and time again when we half filled with water. They always managed to keep the water down, despite the bits of debris that they must have shunted through the disgorging pipes during our three months at sea.

Chay came up with another *bon mot*—'It will soon be all a memory.' That was something I clung on to for the rest of the trip.

The wind on August 30 continued from the Northwest, and we seemed to be screaming along towards home. How we hoped our wives would be on the quay-side in Ireland when we landed.

Chay wanted to have another hour's sleep under the tarpaulin before breakfast. I would have liked that shelter as well, but this was the way we had always managed to operate. When he prayed for more rest, I would be eager to get on. And when I felt I was past all effort and crying for relief, he would say, 'Come on, Number One, there's work to do.' We make a pretty good team, I think. We can rely on each other, and we know that one of us will always manage to get on with the job.

We tried the Sarbe once more at lunchtime that day and were very depressed again to find that no Shackleton arrived. We could not understand this, as the R.A.F. must have had a pretty good idea of where we are in view of the *Finnalpino*'s position report to Lloyd's. They must be very confident of our ability to fend for ourselves, we reflected.

I got another longitude line at five-thirty that day, and this put us about a hundred and twenty miles off Ireland. The position was very satisfactory. We were further north than we wanted, but our intention was still to make for Valentia Island, as this is where we told the *Finnalpino* we would be steering for. If the wind stayed like this we should be on the nail. But if it turned easterly we would pull ourselves by our bootlaces to the centre of Ireland.

It now became necessary to row like mad in any weather, even easterlies, as summer as we knew it when we were further out and to the south had disappeared. We both complained in the mornings of stiff limbs brought on by the cold nights. I wondered if we would catch any night air frosts. I could remember some early frosts at home at the end of August and beginning of September which killed off the last of the summer roses. I hoped that we would not get any, because we now had no extra reserves of strength. The only thing that kept us going now was the knowledge that land and our wives could be only a handful of miles away. As Chay said earlier that morning, 'I'll swim this thing the rest of the way if necessary. We cannot lose now, John.' He was right. We had to make it now.

We spent a very uncomfortable night, but came back to work again on the last day of August determined to really make ground during the day. Of course, the wind shifted. The wind always shifts when you least want it to.

This time it went round South-west to South. This meant that we could no longer keep on our easterly course, and we were crabbed northwards again. The wind rose to a full gale in the afternoon, and it was difficult to row in the seas that got up. They were very short and steep. I supposed that this was because we were getting into shallow water, probably past the hundred-fathom line, and it was a thing to be expected. But they still looked the deep colours of the Atlantic. There was no hint of the browny, greeny seas that you find round the coasts. We still had a way to go.

Chay and I spent all the afternoon sitting under cover and pumping as the shorter seas brought more water into the boat than we expected. By evening the wind went round to South-west. This got us going again, but it was taking us rather fast northwards. I could not see us making Valentia if this kept up.

As we rowed into the evening Chay and I went into details of landing again. This would be a vital part of the trip, and it was necessary for both of us to know the drill word perfect. I regret now that we did not do a practice landing on a beach and on a cliffside back in the States before we left. When it is a matter of survival on land or sea you cannot practise the drills often enough. You find that in a real emergency everything is speeded up and unless you have a properly rehearsed plan you can end up very dead very quickly.

The previous night had added to my anxiety about a cliff landing and was probably the reason that I insisted that Chay and I went over the plan time after time.

I had had a dream. I saw a girl walking down a country lane. In the background was a white cottage, similar to the one in which my wife and I spend holidays in Scotland.

The girl was holding a bundle of uniforms in her arms.

In my dream I looked into the girl's pretty face and asked her, 'Whose clothes are those?'

She averted her eyes and walked right by me without saying a word.

I thought that this was an ominous omen for a cliff landing.

This was the first time that a girl had reached my sub-conscious during the whole of the trip. I did not even dream about Marie-Christine.

Landfall

Chay Blyth: September 1–3

IT was almost over. In a few more days we would reach land triumphantly successful or get smashed to pieces on the rocky coast of Ireland.

John was almost resigned to getting killed, and this disturbed me far more than all the horrors we had gone through in the past three months. I wish now that he had told me about his dream; I might have been able to make those last days of waiting easier for him, for I hate death and have very little time for prophecies and ill omens. There are a million things I have not done yet that I am determined to have a go at before I die.

But John was strangely insistent that at least one of us might drown when we made a landfall, and to save becoming involved in a long discussion on what was for me a sickening subject I agreed to help him prepare two survival kits.

To serve as floats we put together two water-tight containers holding everything we thought we would need, including rations and flares and our precious hoard of film. Then we wrapped our log books in tightly sealed polythene bags and stowed them on top. It was probably the only dry spot on the boat. All day the wind blasted up from the South, and with it came the rain. The clouds seemed to open up, and the water came down in solid sheets. It flattened the waves and bounced back into the air forming a foot layer of mist across the sea.

I was wet all over. My pants rubbed clammily against

my thighs, and the water ran down my arms and legs and into my boots. We took it in turns to row—two hours on and two hours off. I would have liked to have rowed all the time. At least like that I could keep warm.

At noon John took a rough sight which gave our position a little north of 53 North and meant we were less than a hundred miles—possibly within fifty—of the Irish coast.

'I think we're out here for ever,' I said, for about the thousandth time that week. 'If we keep on drifting north we'll end up going right round Ireland and on towards Russia. They'll probably make us heroes of the Soviet Union and give a Moscow parade in our honour.'

'As long as they don't give us any of that kind of treatment in England I shall be happy,' said John.

'Who the hell would turn out to look at us?' I said. 'We look just like a couple of overworked scarecrows. Certainly not hero meat.'

That evening, when the wind dropped and we were gazing over the stern watching the sunset we tried to make a final analysis of our reasons for undertaking this —to most of our friends pointless—journey.

'It has all made sense to me aesthetically,' said John. 'I'm an experience seeker. I'd say that's all we both are —physical experience seekers.

'I was born out of my time. There's no vacancy in this modern age for anyone like me at all. I'm just a dreamer. All one has to be today to survive is a technocrat, which is completely divorced from my kind of life.

'I grew up imagining myself doing things like climbing Everest, or sledding to the South Pole, or canoeing down the Amazon. But most of these things have been done already. By the time I was old enough to try it there were very few things still left to do that didn't require enormous expense or the mounting of a complete expedition. That's really the reason why I chose to do this.'

What John said made sense to me. By now we knew one another very well indeed. It is difficult to disguise one's moods, beliefs and feelings in a boat twenty feet long and six feet wide when one is continually in the other's company.

I knew by now that, like myself, he liked to be faced by a physical challenge. To get one to the point where we were so fatigued that we were lifted out of ourselves and could observe our reactions from a distance as it were, was a kind of triumph. John gets a great sense of elation from being absolutely shattered by exhaustion and then being able to keep on going—to know he can go on endlessly. I get the same feeling. John said it made him almost cry with emotion, to know that he could go on when completely exhausted and find a kind of pleasure in it that he had never experienced in anything else in his life.

'When I was still at school,' he said, 'and discovered that I would never be really good at sports I was quite upset. I don't have a good body, my arms aren't very strong, I'm long in the wrong places and I have sort of funny feet.

'When I was nine years old a shoe salesman took one look at my feet and told my mother they should be reversed. The right one really belongs to the left leg, and vice versa.

'I never had what I always worshipped in an athlete—graceful movement. I got into the first teams in rugby and cricket only by persistence and training. It's because I really wasn't very good that I eventually gave up both sports.'

It is surprising how similar are our feelings in this direction. I have always been a fair swimmer, but that is about all. I suppose if we had had the physical ability we would not have had this mental thing. To both of us finishing is the thing. We excel at tests that make us go on and on. John told me he became captain of boxing at Sandhurst, the Royal Military Academy, only through persistence.

'I was a great loser,' he said. 'I've got some terrific trophies for losing. In one tournament someone broke my nose in an early fight. I won that fight and the next fight, and in the final I came up against a pretty good fellow. My nose was in a poor state by then.

'It was an interesting pain. A sort of sweet sickly smell, and I could hear the bones grate when I was hit. The referee stopped the fight in the last round with one minute to go. It's the only time I was ever stopped, and I had a kind of nervous breakdown.

'I'm ashamed to say that right there in the ring I began to cry and shake. They took me to the dressing room and I just cried and cried. I could not believe that I had been stopped.'

When he finished talking we sat there, silently watching the light brown dorsal fin of a shark following in our wake.

We looked at the swirling currents and the shark's fin slicing through the murky water, and I began to think of the land and my boyhood. My thoughts often dwelt on old, childhood friends, many of whom I had not seen for ten years, and I longed for us all to be together again.

By this time I had long since ceased to marvel at the way John's thoughts so closely followed my own. I was not at all surprised when he began to tell about his days at school: long summer afternoons playing cricket on big side field and fierce muddy rugger matches in the winter; no appreciation of academic values.

Then I told him about fishing with my uncle in Scotland, walking the river bank and then sitting down and

brewing tea, and the scent of the smoke from the burning wood. And so we talked on into the night, with the
smell of the wood smoke right out there in the boat,
each of us drawing word pictures of the places and
things that had brought us the greatest pleasure as children.

Soon after dark a fair breeze from the West sprang up
and we bent to the oars, our minds still filled with
happy childhood thoughts and the knowledge that Ireland and our wives were just below the horizon.

As we rowed we sang one of my favourite songs, which
John now knew by heart.

*The cold wind was howling o'er moor and o'er
    mountain,*
And wild was the search for wha' the lassie might be.
She appeared like an angel in feature and form,
As she asked me the road and the miles to Dundee.

All that night and the next day a good west wind followed over our stern. During my last 'stag' in the dark I
happened to glance over my shoulder and saw the navigation lights of a small boat a few hundred yards ahead
of us.

It was very black and the ship's red, white and green
lights created an eerie effect. A few minutes later I
looked again and found that we had come much closer—
and were in fact on a collision course. The wind was
helping to blow us straight for it.

I shook John awake, and by the time he had taken his
place at the oars we were within five hundred yards of
the other boat. We flashed our torch, but they cannot
have seen it from the bridge, because the trawler passed
right across our bow and only its greater speed averted a
disaster. This was the closest we came to a collision on
the voyage. We did not have our radar reflector erected.

I was not sorry to see it go. The thought of being run down at this eleventh hour made me go cold inside.

Conditions were ideal for rowing, and John decided to stay on the oars. I am glad he did, for it meant he was there to witness one of the most exciting sights of our trip.

Shortly after dawn we spotted a jet trail high in the sky to the West. Gradually as it approached it began to descend, and as it passed overhead we could easily recognise it as a Boeing 707.

We twisted round on our seats and followed its path with loud cheers, knowing that it must be making its descent for Shannon airport. This was the positive proof we needed that land was less than two days away.

At noon John's sighting confirmed that we were, at 11 degrees 25 minutes, only sixty miles from shore. We were rowing now in strong sunshine and had our spare track suits spread across the stern and bow to dry. We intended to wear these for our landing, to look as smart as possible. It was silly really, in view of all the other hazards, to be so concerned about our appearance, but we were very keen to look as unchanged as possible.

'We feel fit and well,' said John. 'And we must look it too. That's important.'

'I don't care,' I told him. 'As long as there's a hot bath and clean sheets waiting for us.'

John laughed. 'Why don't you really do it in style and ride in on the back of one of those?' He nodded to a school of dolphins putting on their own circus display away to our left. Some of the big fish came quite close, and in the clear water they looked like living torpedoes as they streaked at a tremendous pace under the waves.

I said, 'I think I'll wait now until there's something more solid to tread on.' But will I step out, I thought. Or will I end up being hurled out of 'Rosie' against the cliffs. Once again I prayed to God that we might complete our journey safely.

Saturday September 3 dawned grim and grey. The following wind had shifted rapidly to the South and promised to reach gale force before the day was out. I rowed on alone across Galway Bay watching for the planes—out of sight above the low, dark clouds—and tried to work out how many more strokes on the oars were needed to get us to land. Many thousand, I decided, and began to count.

I had reached a hundred when John crawled out from under the canvas hood. He stood up and stretched, then leaned forward to massage the backs of his knees.

A hundred and three, a hundred and four...

Suddenly he blinked and stared at a point just over my right shoulder.

'That's it, over there,' he said, very quietly.

I stopped counting. 'That's what?'

'Land.'

I paused in mid stroke. 'Are you sure?'

'Yes.' He looked again. 'I'm quite certain.'

'Well, I won't look now,' I said. 'I'll look later on when I can tell more distinctly. I don't want to raise my hopes too much, and as I've never been to sea before I wouldn't recognise it.'

It was not a bit like I had imagined it would be. We had tried to keep our emotions in control throughout the trip, but I had expected us to go wild when this moment came. Yet here we were discussing it as though John had just spotted another piece of driftwood in the sea.

However, inside, my stomach was turning over and over, and I had to make a tremendous effort to go on rowing. I was not keen to look in case I could not see it. But the temptation to turn round was very strong.

The decision was taken out of my hands in the end,

because John reported that the weather had closed down and he was no longer able to make out the thin grey line on the horizon.

We rowed on for two hours, and every few minutes John would look back over his shoulder, grin at me and stare out to sea. Then during a slight break in the gale he yelled that he could see land again.

'Look at it. I can make out the shape. I think it's an island.'

I could hold out no longer. Pulling in the oars, I stood up, held on to the Samson post and turned round. I saw the land straight away—a thin line on the horizon.

'Yes,' I confirmed, 'that's land sure enough.'

Neither of us felt real elation at that point, just a relaxed feeling that we were nearing the end of our very long voyage. As we drew closer to Ireland, it became more and more apparent that we had a horrifying landing ahead of us. The gale was building up steadily, dashing great waves halfway up the cliffs that rose straight out of the water.

John took out the chart, and, partly sheltered by the canvas canopy, he tried to pinpoint our position. From our last sighting and the shape of the land ahead we decided that we were approaching a group of islands off the coast of Galway.

'That big one we can see must be Aran,' said John. 'What do you say we make for that?'

I glanced at the watch which was strapped to the thwart.

'We've got about nine hours of daylight left,' I said. 'With any luck we can make it.'

The island of Aran was almost abeam of us to the North, and with the wind blowing hard from the South we decided to make straight for it. Neither of us fancied spending a single night more than we had to in 'Rosie', especially so close to land and in such bad weather.

John took charge of the boat, and we headed due North, pushed from behind by a rising gale. We were now sure that the cliffs we could see were at the centre of Aran Island and decided to make our landfall at one end.

From the chart we knew that there was a lighthouse on one of two smaller islands off the western tip of Aran and, though we could not yet see it, we made this our immediate goal.

Two miles off the main island John shipped his oars and retired to the stern for a further inspection of the charts. We had not come three thousand miles to end up running into a cliff or reef.

After John had made a careful examination of the whole area into which we were heading I set about preparing the packs for an emergency landing. Most of the items we needed were already stowed in the watertight containers. I checked through them to make quite certain we had not forgotten anything—and added a spare watch and compass and a first-aid pack.

As I finished John unfolded his plan of action for discussion.

'Nothing here to worry about. If we can guide her in between Aran and the first of the small islands we should be sheltered from the storm and able to row in easily.'

He said it so matter of factly that it was hard to realise we were about to embark on the most dangerous stage of our journey.

We pulled back the canopy and bundled it against the stern. If everything went the way it should we would not be needing our 'roof' again. And if things went badly, we would not be needing it then either.

By now the gale was so strong that we could see spray blowing almost across the two smaller islands. The gaps between them were only about two hundred yards wide, and we seemed to be rushing towards them. There could be only one attempt.

'We'll have to turn her broadside on,' yelled John. 'I can't control her like this.'

We manhandled the boat round until she pointed sideways towards the outer sound. Every time our stern turned to the sea, we absolutely raced along. We were afraid that we'd miss the gap altogether and crash into the cliffs.

Dashing before the storm, pulling for home, was the second great moment of the trip for John, equalling the elation he felt during the 'white-out'. Once again our fates had been taken out of our hands. He could simply enjoy watching to see what would happen next. We were both singing at the tops of our voices against the howl of the wind. Gradually the details of the cliff became more distinct. The lighthouse rose like a finger pointing from the sea.

We sang 'The Road to Dundee' and another of my favourite songs:

At hush of eventide, o'er the hills beyond the Clyde,
I'll go roving to my haven down in the glen.
The sheep are in the fold, and there's peace worth more
    than gold
In my haven, with my lassie, down in the glen.

As we came in, assessing the gap, we had to make a conscious effort not to fire any kind of flare or rocket, as we did not wish to appear in distress.

The huge Atlantic breakers were smashing into the cliffs with a loud booming roar, sending the torrents of spray leaping across the islands. Our hearts sang with joy at the sheer splendour of it and the knowledge that we had fought a draw with this hungry, cruel sea.

We did make it to the lee of the lighthouse, but the

gale was blowing so hard by then that the waves were coming round both sides of the island and meeting just about where we were. I could well imagine any normal person not wanting to be out in those seas, but we were thrilled, and felt it our due that the sea was giving us such a hard fight, before relinquishing us to the land. It would have been a sorry climax had we rowed ashore in a dead calm.

It took half an hour—perhaps longer—rowing as hard as we could, to make a hundred yards. Gradually we closed the gap between ourselves and the lighthouse, hoping to find a landing platform. The lighthouse keeper, we thought, would make an ideal person to break the news to the mainland and the rest of the world.

By then we were absolutely certain that we were not going to die. We had come all that way, and it just was not going to happen. There was a place to land, but before we could manoeuvre 'Rosie' in two lighthouse keepers appeared and signalled frantically for us to keep away.

They pointed to the east side of the island, and we reckoned they were trying to tell us there was a better landing stage there. It took a further twenty minutes to row seventy feet, and we were beginning to run out of energy. The storm was still rising.

Then the two lighthouse keepers appeared again and waved us towards Aran. We rested on our oars, judging the distance and approach to Aran. The light was beginning to fail, but we calculated we had at least another two hours before complete darkness came.

As we crabbed towards the middle island and then on across the sound towards Aran a sudden heavy rain squall cut visibility to twenty yards, and we lost sight of land. Immediately John hauled in his oars and reached for the latrine bucket.

'I've been wanting to use this for the past hour. Now's my chance,' he shouted.

I must rely on reports I had after reaching Aran to describe what happened next. Apparently the two lighthouse keepers had been keeping an eye on our boat through their telescope. Through the gloom and the heavy rain one saw John reach for the bucket and assumed we were in difficulties. That was when he ordered out the Aran lifeboat.

'They came at your convenience,' I told John later.

Of course at the time we knew nothing about this and were surprised, in view of the appalling weather conditions, to see another boat heading towards us. By this time we were in the lee of the main island and making steady progress along the coast, looking for a harbour to put in.

The seven or eight men on the lifeboat peered over the side as they circled behind us and came abreast. I do not think they had recognised us as the English rowers at that time. Neither of us wanted to be helped even this last little part of the way.

'Ignore them and keep rowing,' I said. So we kept rowing in embarrassment, and the lifeboat crew circled around us in embarrassment.

We smiled shyly back at the sweater-clad seamen as they shouted questions across the ten-foot gap between us. They kept asking us if we wanted a rope, and we decided after ten minutes that we could not just tell them to push off. It was Saturday night, and those fellows had left their families and the warmth of their homes to come out and rescue us. John turned round and grinned at me.

'Whatever are we going to do? We're already virtually home, so does it make all that much difference if we hitch a lift?'

I was still doubtful.

'Won't people say we've cheated?' Somehow I did not care what people thought.

'No. I don't think people will think that. We've already passed the outer islands, and we could land here if we really had to. We've beaten the Atlantic, and that's what we set out to do.'

'Okay, Number One.' I turned towards the boat and signalled for a rope.

So we took the rope and two minutes later had transferred to the lifeboat to break the news to an amazed crew that we had just rowed from the big island—the one three thousand miles away, though later we estimated we had covered nearer 3,500 miles.

It is difficult now, trying to write it just as it happened, to catch the mood of those seven hours as we neared land. I managed to jot rough notes in my log to record the highlights. Here they are:

'The winds built up till it was almost Gale Force. We have been using the jets and props going to Shannon as a guide. We can't be far away now. All day we hear them.

'I was rowing about 09.00 hours; John was making breakfast. He stood up. "Land," he said. I wouldn't look. "I'll wait till we get closer," I said. The weather closed in then.

'We worked out it could only be Aran Island. The rain started to pour down. Both oars come out. We had approx. 9 hours of daylight left. The seas were getting bigger all the time.

'About 14.00 we could make out the Cliffs. I started preparing the packs for an emergency landing. We were both singing now. I believed we hadn't come 3,000 miles to find death on a cliff. We were heading almost N making for the N end of the island to slip round to the leeward side out of the now gale-force wind. The cliffs

were now plain and I could see the sea riding up the
wall.

'Drifted sideways.
Made for Sound.
Cliffs looked like jaws just waiting.
Life jackets on. Life harness.
Kit ready for landing.
Morale high.
Zig-zagging.
Pouring rain.
Quick prayer.
Discussion—I relied on John.
Middle of sound—howling wind.
No place to land on island.
Lighthouse keeper waved us away.
After some extremely hard rowing.
Energy expended.
Made for Aran.
Very heavy rain and wind—bad weather.
Hard work—jerking starting.
Almost to island.
Lifeboat.
Embarrassment.
Good talk.
Father McMann
Wonderful people.
It's all over.
I'm not getting in that boat again for nobody.'

The lifeboat towed us in to Kilronan, and it was there
that we landed. On the quay of the little port a crowd of
locals, children and a few tourists stood huddled under a
naked lamp bulb which stuck out from the wharf.

They were there because they knew the lifeboat had
gone out. They did not know who we were or why we
were being brought ashore. As the lifeboat jarred

against the quay one of the crew shouted our names and a gasp ran round the crowd. They all jostled forward to get a better look at the two mad Paras and their boat.

As we stepped on shore, staggering around a bit and unable to clench our hands for the handshaking, we discovered to our astonishment that we had beaten *Puffin,* which was still somewhere at sea.

And then everyone went mad. The first person we spoke to as we walked off the lifeboat was a Father McMann, the same name as the Father McMann who had blessed the boat back in Cape Cod.

Within an hour we were dressed in dry warm clothes, and suddenly someone pushed a telephone into my hand. I put it to my ear and heard my wife's voice, and at last I knew we were really home.

I think it is best left to John to sum up our adventure. He feels that the whole venture, and the idea behind it, is tied up in a quotation from Shelley which he has written inside his diary:

To suffer woes which hope thinks infinite,
To forgive wrongs darker than death or night,
To defy power which seems omnipotent,
Never to change, nor falter, nor repent.
This is to be good, great and joyous, beautiful and free,
This alone, life, joy, empire and victory.

Authors' note

As this book went to press we heard the news that the *Puffin* had been found upturned in mid-ocean with no trace of her crew, David Johnstone and John Hoare. David Johnstone inspired the idea of our rowing the Atlantic. We should like to pay tribute to the courage of these two men, and we are conscious of a great debt of gratitude for the safe homecoming of *English Rose III*.

Appendix

Our stores and equipment

Navigation

Safety equipment and radio

English Rose III

Track

Cooking, rations and water

Medical pack

Clothing and bedding

Our stores and equipment

In view of the short time available and my belief that simple equipment is more reliable than sophisticated equipment, the lists below are short. However, they were adequate.

Responsibility was divided as follows:

Ridgway

Navigation
Safety
Radio
Seamanship

Blyth

Rations
Medical
Clothing

Navigation

Equipment

Transistor radio (G.E.C. World Monitor) for Washington Time Signal WWV.

Smith's Everest watches

Kelvin Hughes 6-in. Marine Sextant (Micrometer Screw).

Burton's Nautical Tables

Nautical Almanac 1966

Admiralty Chart North Atlantic

Admiralty Routing Charts North Atlantic (June, July and August)

Consol Chart British Isles—transistor radio damaged by sea-water before Consol could be used

Formulae

LATITUDE—Meridian Altitude Sun's Transit (Noon).

Observed altitude ☉	
Index error	————
Apparent altitude	
Total correction	————
True altitude	
Subtract from 90°	————
Zenith distance	
Declination	————
Latitude North	
	════

LONGITUDE—Chronometer Method—8.30 or 15.30 local time. Accurate signals from Washington WWV.

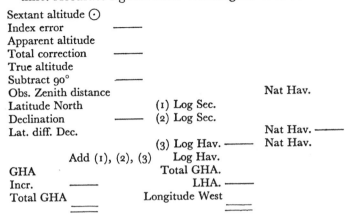

Sextant altitude ☉
Index error ——
Apparent altitude
Total correction ——
True altitude
Subtract 90° ——
Obs. Zenith distance   Nat Hav.
Latitude North   (1) Log Sec.
Declination ——   (2) Log Sec.
Lat. diff. Dec.   Nat Hav. ——
                              (3) Log Hav. ——   Nat Hav.
            Add (1), (2), (3)   Log Hav.
GHA   Total GHA.
Incr. ——   LHA. ——
Total GHA ——   Longitude West ——

Safety equipment and radio

2 × 1 man R.A.F. type liferafts (mainly for psychological reasons)

2 × 1 man airborne type life jackets

2 × 1 man Haward safety harnesses to 20 ft of nylon rope

G.E.C. (U.S.A.) World Monitor Transistor Radio

Lifeline type 610—hand operated—Clifford and Snell Ltd. (never used in correct role for emergency)

S.A.R.B.E. Mk I (never used)

S.A.R.B.E. Mk II (plan to speak with R.A.F. Shackletons not successfully carried out) (Burndept Electronics Ltd., Erith, Kent)

1 × 3 ft parachute type drogue (successful)

1 × 3 ft metal ringed drogue (unsuccessful)

2 × Henderson Diaphragm Mk III T/A Bilge pumps (excellent)

English Rose III

Yorkshire dory built by Bradford Boat Services, Bradford, Yorks.

Specification

20 ft length × 5 ft 4 in. beam
Stem—3 in. × 3 in. iroko
Keel—2 in. × 1 in. mahogany
Hog—3 in. × 1 in. iroko
Chine—3 in. × 1 in. iroko
Frames—3 in. × 1 in. iroko
Double transom—$\frac{3}{4}$ in. marine plywood on hard wood frames. (This is the fitting for outboard motor which we boarded over.)
Gunwale, Rubbing Strakes, Cappings and Outboard Bracket—mahogany.
Skinning—best quality $\frac{3}{8}$-in. marine plywood with all fastenings in brass and copper.

Additions—Aldershot

Turtle decks fore and aft over watertight compartments containing expanded polystyrene. One foot of space below the compartments was left for stowing clothes, wrapped in polythene, and water bags. A false floor was put in to hold 80 gallons of fresh water in 2-gallon liners against the bottom.

Sheathed with Cascover nylon sheathing.

Additions—Cape Cod

Gunwale raised 9 in. and strengthened with oak.
Small cupboards cut into buoyancy compartments.

Rudder fitted.

Four pairs 9-ft ash oars, two pairs 8-ft ash oars with conventional oarlocks.

New thwarts fitted with square (plastic-covered) kapok cushions 1 in. thick.

Theory of buoyancy

1200 lb of fresh water along the bottom of the boat with expanded polystyrene compartments high up at either end of the boat. When capsized the weight of fresh water would tend to twist down and the buoyancy twist up, thus righting the boat. This worked on trial at Southampton. The boat never looked like capsizing on the voyage.

Track

Below are the actual page headings of Captain Ridgway's Log. Points to note are the unexpectedly high incidence of Easterly winds, the changing water temperatures where the Labrador current and Gulf Stream meet and the fact that the position was determined with the use of a sextant only once or twice each week.

Monday June 6
Position—16.00 local 42° 43' N.
                           62° 08' W.
Wind—South-west 4–5

Tuesday June 7
Position—driven North-east over Gulf of Maine
Wind—South-west 5–6
Water temperature—51° F

Wednesday June 8
Position—Gulf of Maine. Row South-east 07.00–18.00
Calm and fog
Water temperature—51° F

Thursday June 9
Position—Gulf of Maine
Course—South-east
Water temperature—52° F

Friday June 10
Position—North end of Georges Bank
Course—South-east
Water temperature—51° F

Saturday June 11
Position—South-east of Gulf of Maine
Course—South-east
Water temperature—51° F

Sunday June 12
Position—South-east of Georges Bank
Wind—South-east Force 3

Monday June 13
Position—South-east Georges Bank
Course—South-east
Wind—South-west
Water temperature—48° F

Tuesday June 14
Position—pushed North-west
Course—Nil
Wind—South-east and East
Water temperature—48° F

Wednesday June 15
Position—41° 13′ N.
          67° 12′ W. at 10.30
Course—South-east
Wind—South Force 3
Water temperature—48° F

Thursday June 16
Position—South-east of North end Georges Bank
Course—South-east
Wind—South-west Force 3
Water temperature—50° F

Friday June 17
Position—South-east of Georges Bank
Course—South-east
Wind—South-east Force 0–2. Fog
Water temperature—50° F

Saturday June 18—Airborne Forces Day
Position—South-east of Georges Bank
Course—South-East
Wind—Nil. Fog
Water temperature—52° F

Sunday June 19
Position—South-east of Georges Bank, *Albatross IV*
        (Woods Hole)
        41° 22′ N.
        66° 15′ W.
Course—East South-east
Wind—o–Force 8. East. Fog half day.
Water temperature—50° F

Monday June 20
Position—off Continental Shelf South-east Georges Bank
Course—East South-east
Wind—Nil. Force 2 South-west
Water temperature—50° F

Tuesday June 21
Position—20.00 70 miles East South-east of
        41° 22′ N.
        66° 15′ W.
Course—East South-east
Wind—Light Variable
Water temperature—54° F

Wednesday June 22
Position—East South-east Georges Bank
Course—085°
Wind—East Force 2
Water temperature—52° F

Thursday June 23
Position—15.30 41° N.
        62° 33′ W.
Course—East
Wind—o–Force 2 South
Water temperature—52° F

Friday June 24
Position—Same
Course—East
Wind—West and East
Water temperature—64° F

Saturday June 25
Position—Same, slipping backwards in wind
Course—Nil (hove to)
Wind—South-east Force 6 all day
Water temperature—64° F

Sunday June 26
Position—14.00 from *Rigoletto* (Bremen)
       40° 55′ N.
       63° 14′ W. (Longitude checked by sight 15.30
       and found accurate ∴ navigation encourage-
       ment.)
Course—East
Wind—East Force 0–3
Water temperature—65° F

Monday June 27
Position—North-east of sun
Course—East
Wind—South and South-west Force 4–6
Water temperature—62° F

Tuesday June 28
Position—North-east of Monday
Course—East
Wind—South-west and West Force 7
Water temperature—68° F

Wednesday June 29
Position—East of Tuesday
Course—East
Wind—South-west and West Force 6–2
Water temperature—69° F

Thursday June 30
Position—41° 33′ N.
         60° 59′ W.
Course—070
Wind—South-west Force 3–5–0
Water temperature—66° F

Friday July 1
Position—41° 48′ N.
         60° 54′ W. *Liquilady* (Monrovia)
Course—South-east
Wind—Nil and South-east South
Water temperature—64° F

Saturday July 2
Position—South-east of Friday
Course—South-east
Wind—East—North—North-west Force 5–6
Water temperature—66° F

Sunday July 3
Position—South-east of Saturday
Course—South-east
Wind—North-west Force 6
Water temperature—74° F

Monday July 4
Position—?
Course—East
Wind—South-west and West Force 5/4–8 and 9
Water temperature—74° F

Tuesday July 5
Position—40° 54′ N.
         56° 01′ W.
Course—070
Wind—South Force 2
Water temperature—66° F

Wednesday July 6
Position—41° N.
            55° 25' W.
Course—East
Wind—South Force 2 and South-west
Water temperature—68°

Thursday July 7
Position—42° N.
            54° 23' W.
Course—East
Wind—South-west Force 4–5
Water temperature—66° F

Friday July 8
Position—42° 30' N.
            53° 39' W.
Course—East
Wind—South-west Force 6–4
Water temperature—69° F

Saturday July 9
Position—43° N.
            51° 30' W.
Course—East
Wind—South-west
Water temperature—59° F

Sunday July 10
Position—43° N.
            51° 14' W.
Course—East
Wind—South-west Force 1–2
Water temperature—66° F

Monday July 11
Position—?
Course—East
Wind—South-east Force 2. Fog
Water temperature—56° F

Tuesday July 12
Position—42° 32·8′ N.
        49° 30·9′ W.
Course—070
Wind—South-west Force 3
Water temperature—60° F

Wednesday July 13
Position—43° N.
        48° W.?
Course—070
Wind—South-west Force 3
Water temperature—61° F

Thursday July 14
Position—43° 10′ N.
        47° 20′ W.
Course—070
Wind—South-west Force 4–5
Water temperature—61° F

Friday July 15
Position—?
Course—East
Wind—South-west Force 7–8
Water temperature—63° F

Saturday July 16
Position—?
Course—East
Wind—South-west Force 7–9
Water temperature—63° F

Sunday July 17
Position—?
Course—East and South-east
Wind—South-west—North-west—North Force 8–5
Water temperature—62° F

Monday July 18
Position—44° 14′ N.
41° 23′ W.
Course—East
Wind—East Force 3-4
Water temperature—? thermometer broken
Tuesday July 19
Position—?
Course—East and North
Wind—East Force 4-5 and South-east Force 4-5
Wednesday July 20
Position—?
Course—North by East
Wind—South South-east Force 4
Thursday July 21
Position—46° 14′ N.
40° 28′ W.
Course—010
Wind—South-east Force 3
Friday July 22
Position—?
Course—North and East
Wind—South-east Force 1-2
Saturday July 23
Position—?
Course—East
Wind—North-east and North
Sunday July 24
Position—?
Course—East
Wind—North-west and North-east
Monday July 25
Position—18.00 (sights) 46° 57·5′ N.
38° 17′ W.
Course—East
Wind—Nil

Tuesday July 26
Position—17.45 G.M.T. 46° 56′ N.
37° 39′ W.
from *Madaket* of New York (West bound).
Note accuracy after 27 days since *Liquilady*.
Estimate 1° longitude per day in calm.
Course—East
Wind—South-west Force 2

Wednesday July 27
Position—?
Course—South-east
Wind—South-east Force 3–6

Thursday July 28
Position—?
Course—South-east
Wind—South-east Force 6–8

Friday July 29
Position—38° W.
47° N.
Course—Nil
Wind—East Force 8–10

Saturday July 30
Position—38° W.
47° N.
Course—East
Wind—West Force 6, South-west Force 9, South Force 9

Sunday July 31
Position—35° W.? (D.R.)
48° N.?
Course—East
Wind—South Force 8–9, South-west and North-west

Monday August 1
Position—34° W.? (D.R.)
48° N.?
Course—East
Wind—West Force 6–8–9–10

Tuesday August 2
Position—32° W.? (D.R.)
          48° N.?
Course—East
Wind—West Force 9–8

Wednesday August 3
Position—?
Course—East
Wind—East Force 2–8

Thursday August 4
Position—17.30 31° 52′ W.
                 47° 00·7′ N.
Course—East
Wind—South-east 1–4–5

Friday August 5
Position—31° 30′ W.? (D.R.)
          47° N.?
Course—East South-east
Wind—North-east Force 4–8

Saturday August 6
Position—31° W.? (D.R.)
          46° N.?
Course—East South-east
Wind—North-east Force 4

Sunday August 7
Position—30° W.? (D.R.)
          47° N.?
Course—080
Wind—South-west Force 1–7

Monday August 8
Position—29° W.? (D.R.)
          48° N.?
Course—080
Wind—South-west Force 5–8

Tuesday August 9
Position—?
Course—East
Wind—East Force 8–4, West Force 3 Calm

Wednesday August 10
Position—47° N.
          27° W.
Course—East by South
Wind—North-west Force 3–4–6

Thursday August 11
Position—47° N.? (D.R.)
          26° W.?
Course—East
Wind—North-west Force 3–4

Friday August 12
Position—47° N.? (D.R.)
          25° W.?
Course—East
Wind—North-west Force 3–4

Saturday August 13
Position—46° 22′ N.
          23° 45′ W. (*Haustellum*) (London)
Course—070
Wind—calm and South-west Force 2

Sunday August 14
Position—47° N.? (D.R.)
          23° W.?
Course—045
Wind—South-west Force 3–5

Monday August 15
Position—47° N.? (D.R.)
          23° W.?
Course—045
Wind—South-west Force 2

Tuesday August 16
Position—47° N.? (D.R.)
22° W.?
Course—045
Wind—South-west—West Force 1–2

Wednesday August 17
Position—47° 30′ N.? (D.R.)
21° W.?
Course—045
Wind—West Force 1 to East Force 5

Thursday August 18
Position—48° N.
19° W.
Course—090
Wind—East Force 2, South-west Force 4–6, East Force
4–6

Friday August 19
Position—48° N.
19° W.
Course—Nil
Wind—East Force 5–6

Saturday August 20
Position—48° N.? (D.R.)
19° W.?
Course—Nil
Wind—East Force 5–6 and North-east

Sunday August 21
Position—48° 30′ N.? (D.R.)
20° W.?
Course—015
Wind—South-east Force 4–5

Monday August 22
Position—49° N.?
20° 30′ W.?
Course—015
Wind—South-east Force 4–5

Tuesday August 23
Position—50° N.? (D.R.)
　　　 20° W.?
Course—055
Wind—South South-west

Wednesday August 24
Position—50° N.? (D.R.)
　　　 20° W.?
Course—055
Wind—South and South-east Force 5–10

Thursday August 25
Position—50° 30' N.? (D.R.)
　　　 19° W.?
Course—050
Wind—South and South-east Force 6–9

Friday August 26
Position—50° 30' N.? (D.R.)
　　　 19° W.?
Course—Nil
Wind—South-east Force 6–8

Saturday August 27
Position—15.00 52° 17' N.
　　　　　　 17° 42' W.
　　　　　　 (M/S *Finnalpino*) (Finland)
Course—075
Wind—South-west Force 1–2, North-east Force 3, North-west Force 3

Sunday August 28
Position—52° 20' N.? (D.R.)
　　　 17° W.?
Course—075
Wind—North-west Force 3–4

Monday August 29
Position—52° 20′ N.? (D.R.)
         16° W.?
Course—075
Wind—North-west Force 5–8

Tuesday August 30
Position—16.30 52° 30′ N.
             14° 34′ W.
Course—075
Wind—North-west Force 6–2

Wednesday August 31
Position—52° 45′ N.? (D.R.)
         14° 34′ W.?
Course—075
Wind—South and South-west Force 4–8

Thursday September 1
Position—53° N.
         12° W.
Course—090
Wind—South-west and South Force 3–8

Friday September 2
Position—53° N.
         11° 30′ W.
Course—East
Wind—West Force 4–6

Cooking, rations and water

Water

Basic requirements 120 gallons for 60 days:

40 × 2-gallon plastic liner
8 × 5-gallon Octopus Plastic Jerry Cans.
In addition 9 × 2-gallon plastic liners full of water were taken to fill up the boat after loading. We were advised to carry 1 gallon of water per day per man and we found that after 32 days we had used only 25 gallons in total.
A solar still was carried in case of emergency.

Rations

We loaded the rations shown below into the boat then filled the remaining space with fresh rations which enabled us to last for approximately 10 days before starting our 60 days' rations.

Rations were packed in individual days and then in polythene boxes of seven days. Much of this was contaminated by sea-water.

BASIC MENUS

Menu 'A'—approx. 2,700 calories per man supplemented by cheese, jam, drinks and goodies.

	Example of water required
6 × packets biscuits	
2 × meat blocks	½ pt
1 × 4 oz precooked rice	⅓ pt
1 × 6 oz beef in curry rice and sultanas	1½ pts
1 × 7 oz fudge no. 18	
2 × Spangles	
4 × Enerzades	
1 × potato mash mix	1 pt
2 × packets instant rice	⅔ pt
2 × packets mixed vegetables	1½ pts
4 × beef cubes	
	5½ pts

Menu 'B'—approx. 2,300 calories, supplemented as in Menu 'A'

6 × packets biscuits
2 × cans sardines
1 × beef in curry rice and sultanas
2 × instant rice
2 × mixed vegetables
1 × diced apples
2 × Smarties
2 × Enerzades
2 × Horlicks tablets
1 × 4 oz precooked rice
4 × beef cubes
2 × Cadbury's chocolate bar

Menu 'C'—approx. 2,500 calories, supplemented as in Menu 'A'

6 × packets biscuits
1 × beef in curry rice and sultanas
1 × fudge no. 18

2 × instant rice
2 × Horlicks tablets
2 × Enerzades
2 × fish bars
1 × 4 oz precooked rice
1 × chicken soup
2 × mixed vegetables
4 × beef cubes
2 × Cadbury's chocolate bar

Menu 'D'—approx. 2,600 calories, supplemented as in
   Menu 'A'
2 × fish bar
1 × apple flakes
2 × dried egg
1 × beef in curry rice and sultanas
1 × oxtail soup
2 × Enerzades
1 × precooked rice
2 × Smarties
2 × Horlicks tablets
4 × beef cubes
2 × rice pudding
2 × Cadbury's chocolate bar
2 oz fudge (sweet)
1 × lemon powder (glucose 1 oz)

Menu 'E'—approx. 2,400 calories, supplemented as in
   Menu 'A'
2 × meat bars
1 × beef in curry rice and sultanas
1 × potato
2 × rice pudding
2 × Horlicks tablets
2 × Enerzades
2 × mixed vegetables
1 × vegetable soup

4 × beef cubes
2 × Cadbury's chocolate bar
2 oz fudge
1 × lemon powder (glucose 1 oz)

SUPPLEMENTARY GOODIES

3 × 1 lb 12 oz jars of peanut butter
2 × 1 gallon orange juice
3 × 1¾ oz pepper
3 × large toothpaste
1 × salt tablet
2 × 4 oz tins of salt
1 × 3 lb chocolate-flavoured tonic drink powder
1 × 2 lb 12 oz coffee
1 × 60 oz skimmed milk
2 oz of sugar per day per man

2 DAYS' RATIONS

(1 pack only) approx. 2,100 calories, supplemented as in
Menu 'A'

2 × sardines
4 × mixed vegetables
1 × mashed potato
1 × dried egg
1 × Batchelor's vegetable soup
1 × oxtail soup
1 × diced apple
1 × precooked rice
4 × beef cubes
4 × Spangles
4 × Smarties
4 × Horlicks tablets
8 × Enerzades
3 × pork bars
1 × beef
2 × Cadbury's chocolate bar

EMERGENCY

		Calories
Verkade	4 × 2 man	20,000
Debren	4 × 1 man	9,900
Horlicks storm	10 × 2 man	50,000
		79,900

Cooking

28 × Bleuet gas cylinders
 2 × Bleuet gas stoves (only one used)
 1 × Prestige Skyline Pressure Cooker
 1 × wooden spoon
 1 × kettle
 1 × set of knives and forks (soon lost in bilges)
 1 × Airborne mug
 1 × aluminium water bottle

Medical pack

Medicine

Multivite vitamin pills (2 each per day) (psychologically
    effective)
codeine tablets
diarrhoea solution (effective)
constipation tablets
throat lozenges
ear drops
eye drops (Optrex)
indigestion tablets
alcohol rubbing liquid (effective)

Drugs

tetracycline and vitamin B pills (very effective for boils)
pethadine
morphia syrettes

Dressings

paraffin gauze (effective for boils)
lint
Elastoplast
bandage
stitching kit and scalpels
butterfly dressings
foot powder (effective)

Creams

calomine compound (effective on salt sores)
Vaseline

lanoline
Johnson's antiseptic cream

Dental—unused

tweezers
forceps
scalpel knife
syringe
excavator
scaler
scissors
local anaesthetic
temporary fillings

Clothing and bedding

Each person

2 × underpants
2 × vests
2 × track suits
1 × pullover
1 × anorak
1 × light rubberised sailing suit
1 × pair Wellingtons
3 × pairs socks (two pairs worn to lessen drawing effect of Wellingtons)

BEDDING

1 × rubber Lilo (soon punctured)
1 × aluminium coated plastic blanket (National Research Corporation) 56 in. × 84 in. (open); 8 in. × 5½ in. (folded); 11 oz.
water bags inflated when empty (very warm)

WETSUITS

Each person was fitted with a Bustersuit

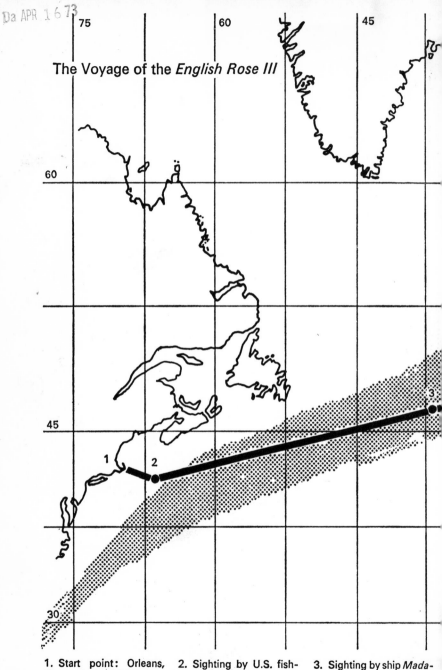

The Voyage of the *English Rose III*

1. Start point: Orleans, Cape Cod: 21.30 hrs. G.M.T., June 4.

2. Sighting by U.S. fishery vessel *Albatross IV*: 7.30 a.m., June 19, at 41° 22′ N., 66° 15′ W.

3. Sighting by ship *Madaket*: 18.00 hrs. G.M.T., July 26, at 46° 56′ N., 37° 39′ W.